TRANSFORMATIVE STUDENT VOICE FOR TEACHERS

TRANSFORMATIVE STUDENT VOICE FOR TEACHERS

A GUIDE TO CLASSROOM ACTION

Dane Stickney, Ben Kirshner,
Carlos P. Hipolito-Delgado,
and Shelley Zion

HARVARD EDUCATION PRESS
Cambridge, Massachusetts

Paperback ISBN 9781682539859

Library of Congress Cataloging-in-Publication Data is on file.

Published by Harvard Education Press,
an imprint of the Harvard Education Publishing Group

Harvard Education Press
8 Story Street
Cambridge, MA 02138

Cover Design: Endpaper Studio

The typefaces in this book are Latienne, Agenda, and Avenir Next.

We dedicate this book to brave teachers, the ones willing to interrogate themselves, change the curriculum, tackle real problems, and position youth to lead the way.

Contents

Foreword

I am not new to Transformative Student Voice (TSV). For the past seven years, I have used the curriculum and pedagogical approach in my social studies and leadership classes at a public "pathways" high school that caters to students who have struggled in traditional high schools. These young people have often experienced trauma, both inside and outside of school. TSV is an exceptionally strong way to position students as important and elevate their lived experience as powerful sources for research and inspiration for action. I came to TSV through my relationship with this book's lead author, Dane Stickney. Dane supported me through my teacher licensure and master's studies at the University of Colorado Denver. He saw many similarities between my work and the tenets of TSV, taking every opportunity to encourage me to pursue TSV training. The man would not leave me alone, and eventually he succeeded in recruiting me to join a student voice and leadership program sponsored by my district. I never could have imagined the journey that ensued.

As you'll learn in this book, the TSV approach is straightforward enough. TSV positions youth to build community, identify a problem, conduct their own research, develop policy, and try to get that policy enacted. Attempting to do that in a real high school classroom is certainly an adventure, but it's an adventure worth taking. A year ago, students and I tackled the issue of resource inequities between traditional and alternative school settings. Seeing those students utilize the TSV approach to center a topic that mattered to them and present it to the district on their terms was a powerful experience that the students and I will never forget. In the end the students created a policy narrative. They described themselves as the "mess-ups, the bad kids, the throwaways" but stressed that they "still deserve a well-rounded and equal education." TSV gave us the tools to rise above the labels, stereotypes, and trauma and instead focus on the young people's hopes, dreams, and actions. Collectively, that did wonders for the youth who engaged in TSV. They felt confident, like they had become experts at something, and that their actions mattered.

While that was obvious in the moment and will become more apparent as you read the book, with TSV, the less visible moments are sometimes the most powerful. Let me take you behind the scenes of my classroom and share one small story. Marie (a pseudonym) was a particularly shy junior student. Having just arrived at our school earlier that month, she clung to her friend who had been with us for several years, seeking safety as a permanent background character. In our class, though, we don't *do* background characters. I remember when I first told her that she needed to start preparing a lesson that would be delivered to her student peers. Marie held the role as one of our community's lead facilitators, and teaching content relevant to our research was among her assigned duties. In the time she had been with us, her voice had yet to rise above a discernible whisper, but she would now be tasked with teaching others some key TSV skills, including root cause analysis, where students frame problems as a tree, its symptoms as leaves, and causes as roots. This important frame helps young people realize that *they* are not the source of the problem; its true roots usually connect to social or historical issues. There is power in youth being able to shift their critical gaze from themselves to the systems around them. When it came time to deliver the lesson, Marie's voice was shaky, her face buried in the notecards that told her precisely what she was supposed to say. It was by no means a marvel of teaching, nor did the task fit neatly within her displayed skill set. But student leadership is a necessary part of TSV. If each young person has an important and individualized role within the greater research project, they are more engaged, and the entire group functions better.

While important, her leadership in the moment was not the most powerful part of the interaction. Several months later, during Teacher Appreciation Week, Marie offered me a small gift that included a thermos and a handwritten note. She thanked me for my investment in her growth, stating, "I would have never come out of my shell as quickly without you." And I would have never been able to support her in that way without TSV. By relinquishing the power I traditionally held as the teacher and intentionally seeking out opportunities to challenge students' preconceived notions of self, the young people learned to embrace their own capacity to hold power in ways they had not done before. Pushing Marie to regularly lead class allowed her to see herself in a different light. The goal was never to make her the perfect facilitator, though her skills would naturally improve the more she used them. Instead, it was about providing a platform that gave her the opportunity to try something new and believe that she could do it.

This was the point.

If we have the expectation that our young people will one day lead in critical fronts, we have to let them start trying now. The TSV curriculum and pedagogical approach provides engaging and rigorous ways to do that with students. *Transformative Student Voice for Teachers: A Guide to Classroom Action* starts inside a teacher's head and heart. While the TSV skills can be developed, there is no shortcut for doing important internal learning and unlearning *before* engaging with youth. The process then shifts to engaging young people in critical conversations about their lived experience. This important dialogue helps move students toward choosing a meaningful topic to investigate. With that problem clear, the book investigates root cause analysis, the very activity that Marie led with her peers. That sets the stage for putting the R into YPAR (Youth Participatory Action Research)—learning research methods and analysis. After young people have done things like conduct surveys, interview peers, and meet with adult power players, they dream a policy and share it in a public space. This is where TSV really shines. The book ends in a more theoretical space that dovetails nicely into the more academic companion book, *Transformative Student Voice: Partnering with Young People for Equitable School Improvement,* though both can be used independently.

You'll learn about the TSV process in depth in the coming pages. Trust me—and trust Marie—TSV is a powerful approach that makes the act of schooling much more enjoyable for students and, as has been my case, teachers. TSV has helped me revolutionize my practice. I consider the authors of this book mentors, colleagues, and friends. I hope you can find as much comfort and support in the TSV process as the students and I have.

Darrell Hopson,
Educator, Denver
Public Schools

SECTION ONE

Introduction

THE AUTHORS OF THIS BOOK DEVELOPED the idea of Transformative Student Voice (TSV) with the goal of starting a youth revolution, one that centers the voices of young people in school reform and transformation. We started with a wondering: *What would it look like if young people used their power to transform schools and communities?* That question has sparked our work in the arena of youth development and empowerment for more than fifteen years. Along the way, we've witnessed many powerful moments. TSV work often culminates with youth delivering policy presentations. High schoolers of different races, ethnicities, home languages, and countries of origin take the stage together in small groups to present policies demanding equitable change in their schools and communities. This has looked like pregnant and lactating mothers, who are also students, asking for more calories in their school lunches. Or middle schoolers presenting to local politicians a plan for safer streets after a tragic accident. Or young women in an area charter school requesting free tampons and menstruation products. Or a cross-district team of young Black and Latine leaders demanding that police be removed from school grounds.

The presentations often follow a similar flow: some sort of intro that captures the audience's attention before moving to introductions and sharing research and policies. One of the most powerful presentations we've witnessed included high school students wearing paper labels with hurtful comments from teachers written on them. A Latina's label read, "Not smart enough for AP classes." A young Black man's read, "My teacher said she gets nervous when I smile." The students then introduced themselves. After presenting a research-informed policy, including student-designed and student-facilitated cultural competence training for teachers, the youth tore up the papers, declaring that they were more than their labels. The youth left the stage hyped, hugging each other, hugging their teacher, and jumping up and down. It's this moment—elation, community, pride—that fuels us in this work.

While the presentations or outputs are the most public moments of the TSV approach, the process is perhaps even more rewarding. But it's hard to see and even harder to emulate. We know educators want their students to experience agency and belonging in their classrooms and communities like we describe above; they want academic learning to be relevant to students' everyday lives and consistent with values of social justice and human dignity. Too often, however, top-down leadership, assessment mandates, and lack of professional development makes support for student voice and agency a distant goal. This youth-first approach sounds good, but it becomes secondary to educators who are just keeping their heads above water. Further, teachers who do engage in critical action-oriented pedagogies tend to feel alone and unsupported.

In response, our team has developed this guidebook for teachers focused on *how* to craft a classroom community that organizes student learning around cycles of critical reflection, inquiry, and action—what we call Critical Civic Inquiry (CCI). (TSV refers to a broad array of schoolwide practices; CCI is the curriculum we have developed for facilitating student-driven action research.) Three of the authors—Ben, Carlos, and Shelley—came together around 2008 to draw on their individual experiences to create curricular and pedagogical approaches that centered youth voice through meaningful partnerships with adults and inquiry into real problems that young people faced. Ben is a youth organizing expert who has researched and written about youth voice and agency from a variety of angles. Carlos has a background in school counseling and was initially drawn to youth voice work to increase critical consciousness in students and promote identity development. He has since become more interested in youth sociopolitical development—how young people take action to positively impact their schools and communities. Shelley's work focuses on diversity, equity, and inclusion as well as school reform that implicates adults as important partners for change. In fact, Shelley, Carlos, and Ben have coauthored a companion book to this one about the theory of TSV and adults' role in it, titled *Transformative Student Voice: Partnering with Young People for Equitable School Improvement.*[1] Dane took a master's level class about CCI from Ben, Carlos, and Shelley in 2010, and his classroom served as one of the early, foundational sites of their research. He has since moved on to work in teacher education, and he wrote his PhD dissertation about CCI. All four authors believe CCI is applicable to *all* school subjects—not just civics—by facilitating inquiry projects about issues that matter to students and enabling students to act based on what they learn.

We draw on fifteen years of teacher and district partnerships, published peer-reviewed research, and decades of leading educator training—taking teachers through the practical steps required of a CCI cycle along with warning them about barriers that can get in the way. Each chapter showcases a specific, real-world application of CCI, identifies challenges and common traps, and provides evidence of the process's impact. While you'll hear from us in each chapter, we'll also feature tips and insights from students and educators who have been through the process.

Section 1 is where it all begins, with some prework about adult and teacher self-awareness. Section 2 focuses on beginning this work with students, which includes developing relationships and trust. Section 3 shifts toward empowering youth to work in groups to conduct research about problems in their schools and communities. Section 4 looks at youth claiming power and voice related to the problem they are investigating. Finally, section 5 examines how young people and adults can work together to sustain equitable change.

Back to the beginning, we know what you're thinking: *Prework? Sounds optional.* Skip out on this at your own peril. Facilitating action research with your students requires parallel leaps of adult development: humility, listening, self-awareness, courage, and awareness of power and privilege. In other words, reflecting on your biases, hopes, and fears. As much as CCI is about youth development, you will also be pushed to grow, on parallel tracks, as a human and educator. Moreover, you will want to organize allies among your colleagues as you set out on this journey.

ONE

Self-Awareness

DANE, AN AUTHOR OF THIS BOOK, had a terrible first year teaching middle school. The thought of returning for a second year of meeting status-quo demands, like prioritizing test scores and giving demerits for uniform infractions, seemed miserable. Instead, he wanted to focus on the more relational aspects of teaching and the more exciting ideas of youth agency and student voice.

Something, Dane knew, needed to change. And it wasn't his students. And it probably wasn't going to be the big, heavy US school system with its gaze on testing and compliance. Dane knew something in himself and his practice needed to shift. He enrolled in a master's program and signed up for a class called Critical Civic Inquiry (CCI), taught by this book's coauthors, Ben, Shelley, and Carlos. Dane thought he was merely pushing his pedagogy and curriculum development. What he didn't realize at the time was that the CCI process would launch him on an unsettling but eventually deeply rewarding process of unlearning what he thought were the traditional ways of teaching while learning new ways to center youth voice and agency. While this chapter focuses at points on Dane, it is meant to bring into focus the learning—*and unlearning*—required for adults to help craft student-centered spaces. Future chapters will feature vignettes from different teachers who have engaged with CCI.

UNLEARNING THE NARRATIVE OF SCHOOLING

Dane grew up attending traditional public schools that controlled students' noise level, where they sat, what they ate, when they used the bathroom, what they learned, and how they were allowed to express those new understandings. Often, this *narrative of schooling,* or what school is "supposed to be," promotes practices that get in the way of democratic and humanizing modes of instruction. Professional benchmarks for teachers and standardized measures for assessing student learning reinforce this story of schooling, essentially incentivizing teachers to prize things like academic growth and compliance over skills like critical consciousness and leadership.

Beyond that, the teaching profession has become deeply focused on educators observing *exemplars*, or models of a certain educational approach, and then translating them to their own context—think restorative conversations or Socratic seminars. Teachers learn about the theory, see an example, and attempt to enact it themselves. The CCI approach asks teachers to do something unusual: share power with students and support young people in identifying a social justice issue, conducting their own research around it, developing more just policy solutions, and eventually presenting those ideas to adults in power. Educators don't often get to observe models of classrooms that prioritize student voice in this way, and CCI is a process that takes time and is hard to see fully in one activity or lesson.

Teachers embarking on CCI must be brave, choosing a path that traditional schooling doesn't necessarily support or accept. Dane, certainly, held privileged identity markers that insulated him from harsher recourse from his administration. Other teachers may *not* be in that situation, and they should certainly weigh their own job safety and security when teaching against the status quo. Regardless of the context, before even entering a classroom or engaging in curricular activities, teachers must do deep reflective work. As Dane often asked himself: *what of my teacher self needs to change (or be unlearned altogether) to allow for a new, more liberatory vision of school to flourish in my classroom?*

RACE, POWER, AND PRIVILEGE

Dane's journey into deeper self-awareness began with reading about race, power, and privilege.[1] Several books or articles could serve this purpose, but the key for Dane was thinking of himself and his students as humans with ever-shifting identities, each identity having some degree of power. The National Center for Education Statistics reported that in 2020–21 the American public school teaching force was 80 percent white, while student demographics are closer to 50 percent white.[2] In other words, the teaching force is overwhelmingly white while the student population is not, leading to an imbalance of white teachers. Dane—a white, cisgender male—for the first time began to deeply realize that much of his power in the classroom and beyond was *unearned*. His gender identity, race, fluency in English, and more opened certain opportunities and afforded respect that people with other identity markers don't necessarily receive. Dane grew up with access to a family farm in the Midwest, and the readings encouraged him to think more specifically about how his identity and family history empowered him. The theme of colonization was easy to see, as the land his family had profited from for decades originally belonged to the Pawnee tribe. Many of Dane's ancestors acquired social capital by serving in the US military. Together, Dane could see how colonization and militarization had set his family up to succeed in the US capitalist structure. He hoped he could interrupt that reliance on forceful taking and sustain something more humanizing with his students. This gave him clear and specific things to unlearn and patterns to break in the classroom. Below are some statements and questions he crafted:

- My family, my people, have profited from taking. How can I unlearn those ways, and focus more on sharing and creating with students?
- My family, my people, have gained social capital through militarized othering, violence, and fear. How can I, instead, help generate trust, healing, and community with students?
- My family, my people, have been active in and supported the capitalist dehumanization of ourselves and others. How can I reject commodification of myself and young people and instead honor our individual identities, collective histories, lived experiences, and dreams?

While Dane's statements and questions may not be relevant to you and your contextualized identity, this line and depth of thinking is important for educators looking to lead a student-centered learning space.

Some guiding questions to consider:

- Which of my various identities carry unearned power?
  - Think about race, gender, ethnicity, ability, citizenship status. When thinking along racial or ethnic lines, get specific. Instead of "white," for example, consider something like "Scots-Irish" or "German from Russia."
- Which of my various identities carry earned power?
  - Think of things like degrees and certificates, but also expertise, accomplishments, and lived experience.
- How do others see me?
  - In what ways are my identities marginalized, judged, or punished by others?
  - In what ways might I intimidate others?
- What patterns am I trying to disrupt or what goals am I trying to achieve?
  - What family or personal histories do I want to interrupt?
  - What systems that have impacted me or my family need resisting?
  - What personal traits, mindsets, or biases do I need to change for me to be my best self for students?

COUNTERING ADULTISM

Age is another major area where Dane and other adults are given unearned power. John Bell describes adultism as "behaviors and attitudes based on the assumption that adults are better than young people, and entitled to act upon young people without their agreement," and states that it is "reinforced by social institutions, laws, customs, and attitudes."[3] Some of the more notable instances of adultism in schools, according to Bell, include teachers being able to yell at students when the opposite would result in discipline; youth being punished when they express frustration; teachers grading students but rarely giving students the opportunity to grade teachers; and, typically, schools not providing avenues for youth to have a say in school decisions.[4] Educators must actively work against the inclination to *do unto* youth. Of course we need to intervene if young people are actively harming themselves or others, but we need to consider where the line of intervention exists for ourselves as educators and the context in which we work. It is essential to consider how we treat young people, and whether we consider them to have agency and be deserving of respect and dignity as humans. Bell offers a variety of guiding questions when reflecting on potential adultist behavior.

Bell suggests adults ask themselves the following questions when reflecting on interactions with youth.

Would I . . .

- Treat an adult this way?
- Talk to an adult in this tone?
- Grab this out of an adult's hand?
- Make this decision for an adult?
- Have this expectation for an adult?
- Limit an adult's behavior in this way?
- Listen to an adult friend's problem in this same way?[5]

These questions forced Dane to, among other things, deeply consider his role in the school's behaviorist management system, which required students to walk on taped lines on the floor, adhere to a strict dress code, and sit and respond in regimented ways. He could not think of an instance when he would treat adults in such ways. (The carceral system, perhaps, is one arena where adults control each other to this degree.) Dane decided to take some risks. Some were small, like allowing students to sit in circles, not in neatly formed rows and columns of desks. Some were bigger, like supporting students in connecting academic learning to their lived experience.

When the class topic turned to undocumented student access to college, Dane's classroom became a place where young people shared passionately about bad things that had happened to them in school and beyond, and they used those experiences as fuel to dream of more equitable policies and approaches. Thinking about adultism made Dane reflect on how much he talked and how little he listened to his students. To change that, he rejected some of the school's expectations of students sitting silently, raising their hands, and only speaking when called upon. In Dane's class, they weren't raising their hands. They were authentically building off each other's ideas and even pushing back on each other at times. It sounded more like a kitchen table than a classroom. While Dane was excited, his principal was not, eventually threatening his job if he didn't meet more school expectations. Inspired by the students, Dane negotiated with his principal. In the end, despite some changes, Dane was allowed to proceed partly because his classes put up strong interim test scores. It took courage not only to interrogate his own adultist ways but even more to stand up to his principal and the school's rigid systems.

That's what Dane did; what would you do? As an adult, it's important to balance sharing your own important and valuable knowledge and experiences while allowing young people a space to do that same. Doing some thinking about this *before* entering the classroom is paramount.

EDUCATOR EXAMPLES

Dane's prework—which proved an ongoing, reflexive practice—allowed him to share power by leading with humility and having specific goals from his personal and family history. He built trust by shifting classroom expectations to allow students to more freely share themselves. He also deeply listened to what they had to say and made personal connections of his own when appropriate. This is not the only way to build self-awareness and use it as a lever to build learning spaces with youth. Following are some examples of how other educators have built in space and time for personal reflection, both before implementing the CCI curriculum and on an ongoing basis.

Lucy, a middle school science teacher, brought a wealth of experience and credentials to the classroom—an Ivy League degree, years of social justice engagement, and support from a prestigious national teaching organization. None of that meant much to her students, mostly native Spanish speakers living below the poverty line. Lucy's main task was earning her students' trust.[6] Lucy deployed a seemingly simple approach: engage in dialogue with her students and, most importantly, listen. A classroom conversation about problems at the school resulted in an uncomfortable moment when a student resisted talking about his school's inferiority. He kept repeating, "Why are we talking about this?" He questioned his teacher's critical stance and expressed hurt from the piles of data labeling the school and its students as inferior. Lucy used that moment to keep listening and allow youth questions and concerns to guide the project. Things finally clicked when Lucy and the students went on a visit to a more affluent school to compare resources. The youth, again, engaged in difficult conversations about what they saw, but this time Lucy played more of a backup role, listening and offering support when necessary. In the end, Lucy's impressive background wasn't the difference-maker for the students; her self-awareness and willingness to talk less and listen more is what won them over.

Mark, a fifty-year-old, white, English language development teacher, presents a stark contrast to his students—high schoolers from Mexico, El Salvador, and Guatemala, among other places. Instead of pretending to be someone else, Mark chose to be as authentic as possible with his students. Specifically, he reflected on past experiences where power and privilege were on his side.[7] As a soda deliveryman, he was given more money and better routes than his coworkers of color. While teaching in remote Alaska, he was starkly aware of being of a different race and culture; *he* was the outsider. While living in Central America, he again felt ostracized despite buying land and attempting to become part of the community. To build rapport with his students, Mark reflected deeply on his experiences and how they impacted the youth in his classroom. He and the students also began to explore these kinds of life experiences in class, writing a narrative essay with identity charts, life maps, and readings about race and culture. This also gave Mark important information about his students that he leveraged to deepen relationships. Had Mark not engaged in this deep personal reflection around his own power and privilege, however, he might well have felt yet again like an outsider, this time with his students.

With more than ten years in the classroom, Emily's practice was tight and effective: clear objectives, tried-and-true activities, strong assessment and feedback practices. She had to question it all, however, when she started engaging in Transformative Student Voice. She structured a get-to-know activity in which students were supposed to put themselves in order by birthdate. Only one young man spoke, asking everyone about their birthdates. Few students responded or participated. The extreme awkwardness troubled Emily; *if they can't talk about birthdays, how are we going to share power with one another?*[8] She prompted the students to return to their seats for a reflective writing activity—through which students shared that they didn't participate because they didn't know or trust anyone in class. The youth shared that they were used to the teacher telling them what to do; they hadn't had experience working with peers to figure something out. Emily listened and acknowledged their concerns. She then shared videos and readings about vulnerability, which sparked student connections to the ideas of authenticity and shame. Over the course of the year, the students became more comfortable and empowered in the space. It flourished during one conversation about police presence in the school. One young man shared powerful and hurtful experiences with law enforcement in his past. Another student chimed in. Soon, the youth were leading a deep and meaningful conversation about problems in their school. Emily, the teacher, sat silently in the circle, listening. While that may sound like a passive stance, Emily had actively and intentionally adapted her practice and pedagogy after deeply reflecting on the needs and strengths of students in her classroom.

TIPS FOR BUILDING YOUR OWN SELF-AWARENESS

- Learn about your own family history and background.
- Interrogate the relationship between your identities and earned and unearned power.
- Focus, specifically, on the unearned power adults typically hold over youth.
- Consider patterns in your personal and family history you'd like to interrupt.

(For a variety of resources, visit TransformativeStudentVoice.net.)

WHAT TO AVOID AT THIS STAGE

- *Punishing past actions.* As you learn new things about yourself, you will likely regret your previous actions or words. While reflection is good, don't dwell in the past. Being mired in guilt helps no one.
- *Stopping at mindset.* Avoiding past mistakes isn't just going to magically happen. As the mindset shifts, so, too, should our actions. Set goals and establish routines to ensure you're making the types of changes you intend.
- *Doing too much.* You may decide several things need to shift. Tackle them in stages or chunks. As Ben often advises, think about "tinkering" with your practice—try new things and pay attention as you go.

CONCLUSION

Key Takeaways

- Deepening your self-awareness is necessary for leading students through the CCI curriculum.
- A good place to start is reflecting on your own identity markers and the corresponding power that may or may not come with them (race, age, power, privilege).
- Self-awareness can look different for educators with varying identities and contexts, but it should always be done in the act of *learning* or *unlearning* to deepen relationships with students.

Up Next: Forming Authentic Partnerships

Now that you've done some deep personal reflection about your identity, and specifically your role as an adult, it's time to move away from the traditional dynamics of control and power in schools and think about partnering with youth.

FIGURE 1.1 **Beginning the process**

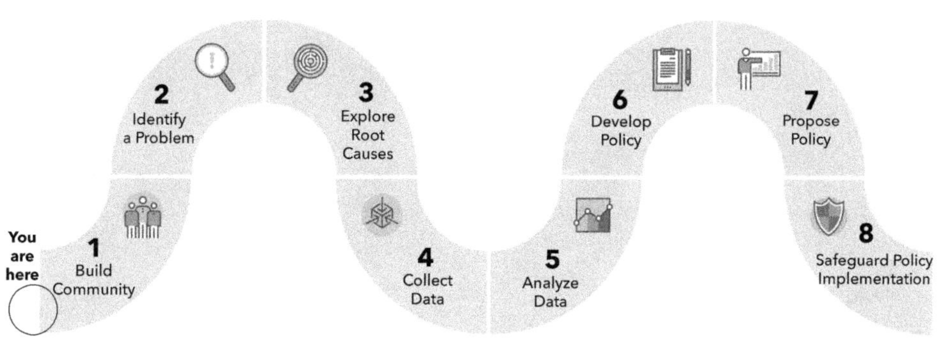

SECTION TWO

Getting Started with Your Students

STUDENT ACTION RESEARCH PROJECTS build on young peoples' lived experiences as an entry point to identifying a problem. The process quickly expands on those lived experiences, as youth collect data, learn about social systems, engage in youth-adult partnerships, and propose and implement solutions. But teachers need to earn trust and build norms for communication in order for students to feel ready to be vulnerable and bring more of themselves into the classroom. This section explores how to cultivate this kind of classroom community, navigate conflicts that can arise, and avoid traps around consensus decision-making. This section will address a set of key elements to getting started with students.

TWO

Forming Authentic Student-Educator Partnerships

DURING SUMMER TRAINING OPPORTUNITIES and through professional development sessions, Raymond had deepened his already strong self-awareness of his identity as a Black high school social studies teacher. As he prepared for his second year of teaching a class called Student Voice and Leadership, he had also taken the new step of developing allies (we will discuss this at length in chapter 12), most specifically the chair of his social studies department, who strongly supported Raymond's desire to focus on young people's agency and leadership skills. Now it was time to actually get started implementing Critical Civic Inquiry (CCI) with his students. That, Raymond knew from the prior year, is harder to do than it sounds. Specifically, Raymond felt that his students at New Outlook Academy—a *pathways* high school, meaning it focuses on credit recovery and serves students who have been forced out of other schools—had never truly claimed ownership over the class the previous year. He had asked them to identify a problem, conduct their own research, and devise more equitable policy solutions, but on reflection, he realized that he and his students hadn't yet practiced the art of sharing power, which is central to a healthy student-teacher partnership.

Developing youth-adult partnerships is fundamentally a relational approach to teaching. Teachers view their students as partners in the education journey and share power accordingly. In a partnership approach, teachers need to unlearn the idea that students are there to be disciplined or fixed. They invite students to bring their whole selves into the classroom. Educators also share something of themselves; they locate themselves for their students. This connects to what Sepehr Vakil and Maxine de Royston call *politicized trust*, "the development of respectful and mutually reciprocal relationships" between teacher and students, including "understanding each other," "respect for one another," and "solidarity with one another."[1] When teachers and students are free to be vulnerable with each other, they can form authentic relationships, ones not dictated by behavior plans or nourished with extrinsic rewards. This is when trust flourishes and power can truly be shared. Because such efforts counter business as usual in American public schools, this process requires intentional practice and learning by teachers and students. The next sections share specific strategies from different educators, starting with Raymond, about how they've formed authentic youth-adult partnerships.

LEADERSHIP ROLES

To more intentionally create partnerships with his students through sharing power, Raymond worked with them to ensure that everyone had an important leadership role in keeping the work of the class moving forward. Raymond had an interesting advantage that many teachers don't have: his class consisted of students across grade levels, and students could take his class for more than one year if they wanted. Using a consensus protocol (see sidebar), the class elected two upperclass students to serve as leads. The leads focused on monitoring team progress, assigning tasks as needed, and serving as representatives at district meetings. Two other students filled the role of logistics and workflow coordinators; they focused on creating agendas, taking notes, organizing files, and creating a long-term calendar. Another pair of students served as community buddies, conducting daily well-being check-ins with peers. Students also filled other roles, including community liaisons, lead researchers, and lead facilitators.

CONSENSUS-MAKING PROTOCOL FROM THE CCI CURRICULUM

When making a decision:

- Create a list of choices (in slides, on the board, on chart paper).
- For each, engage in a discussion and cite evidence from any work or research you've done so far:

    - Can you live with us making this choice?
    - Can you support your peers in researching it?
    - Can you commit to being part of this problem's solution?
- After the discussion, eliminate options where people answered no to the above, hopefully homing in on two or three choices.
    - Rate each remaining choice: 1. Love it; 2. Like it; 3. Meh; 4. No way.
- Discuss the ratings, eliminating choices until consensus is reached.
  Remember: consensus means everyone must be able to live with the choice.

Ensuring that each role had two students assigned was an intentional decision by Raymond. He taught at an alternative high school where regular attendance was a challenge for many students. Ideally, the students would work together. In a pinch, however, at least one of the two was almost always in class. He also approached leadership as a learning opportunity, not a reward, as is sometimes the case with status-quo schooling (for example, class presidents, prom queens, and appointed student councils). Raymond trusted his students not only to fulfill their roles but to develop skills that would hopefully grow throughout the year and make sharing power not only easier but more natural.

While these specific leadership roles worked for Raymond's classroom, you might devise others for your classroom context. What matters is giving young people a chance to lead in a more sheltered environment and with more manageable boundaries. While Raymond used pairs, small groups with assigned roles can achieve similar means. These roles could be basic (facilitators, timekeepers, recorders, materials managers) or more specific to the process (survey designers, schedulers, field researchers, and analysts).

Across these different examples, we recommend that you, the teacher, work with students to develop clear expectations of the roles and how to execute them. Consider modeling what different roles look like and then asking for feedback from the students about what worked and didn't. You can have fun with this—try modeling a terrible facilitator who answers their own questions or calls on people when they're not ready. Your students will get it, and they can use your "bad example" to generate some guidelines for good facilitation.

ACTS OF VULNERABILITY

Nader had no idea how to tell his middle school students what had happened to him during the summer.[2] The eighth-grade social studies teacher still couldn't believe it himself. He had been out dancing with his two roommates. When they left the club, they waited at a crosswalk, the light turned green, and they entered a major four-lane street. Halfway across, Nader heard an engine roar. He barely had time to jump out of the way as a car sped by, running the red light. The car struck Nader's roommate, killing him instantly. On the precipice of enacting the CCI curriculum, Nader's work around self-awareness convinced him he couldn't hide this tragedy from his students. On the first day of class, Nader set up an *ofrenda,* or altar, to his friend. He told the students his story and invited them to bring in items or pictures to honor people they had lost in their own lives.

The altar soon overflowed, and the youth began asking more questions about the accident. They got angry. It wasn't fair, they said. Something should be done, they demanded. The class launched into the CCI curriculum, splintering into groups examining different sub-issues of the problem: Are speed bumps allowed on the street? How much do roundabouts cost? Why isn't there a permanent rideshare station near this busy nightlife area? What if they reduced the number of lanes from four to three? Is it possible to have pedestrian-only hours? While this is an example of a *teacher's* lived experience sparking a conversation about a social problem, the youth still made the project their own. Students spent their lunches videoconferencing with elected officials, devoted class time to meet in person with a city councilman, and stayed in weekly contact with a major rideshare executive. In the end, the city adopted several of their proposals, and Uber installed a permanent rideshare station in the area. As pleased as Nader was with the class's civic impact, the connection he had formed with his students was what made him truly proud.

Although Nader's vulnerability about the painful loss of his friend galvanized his class, teacher vulnerability does not require a traumatic event to be impactful. Vulnerability just means locating yourself for your students and being less opaque and more real for them. Our partners in a student voice program encourage their teacher-coaches to facilitate a mask activity. Young people, as well as the teacher, pair up and create papier-mâché masks of each other's faces. Once dried, they then decorate each side of the mask. The inside represents how the person views themselves. The outside represents how they think others view them. The students and teacher then sit in a circle and share their masks. Almost always, they get emotional. Less personal activities can also be generative. During the COVID-19 pandemic, we observed a teacher use a scavenger hunt during a video class meeting with strong results. She asked the students to find something blue. One student came back with a common blue cereal bowl. Another student shared that they had the same bowl. Soon, screens that had remained dark for months popped on, each with a smiling face holding a blue bowl. The teacher participated, as well, showing off a shiny blue bowl from her own cabinet.

Our colleagues at the Public Science Project, Madeline Fox and Michelle Fine, describe an activity that we have also found useful in our participatory work with youth.[3] Called *To whom are you accountable?*, this is an activity where the facilitator shares a brief letter they have written to someone or some people—it could be an ancestor, it could be a child, it could be a collective. The letter conveys who you feel accountable to in your work and why. Then the facilitator invites students to write their own letter to someone they feel accountable to for the action project they are soon going to launch. Sharing these letters can help build trust within the group and ground people's commitments to the work. Whether intricately planned or spontaneously started, activities that allow adults and young people to be vulnerable together are necessary parts of the CCI process.

COMMUNITY RITUALS

"Come on guys, we must do *In Lak'ech!*" said Kimmie, a student in a high school leadership course. She and her classmates then engaged in call-and-response reading of a five-line section of the bilingual poem *Pensamiento Serpentino*.[4]

A native Spanish-speaking student started: "Tú eres mi otro yo." The class repeated the words in chorus. Then Kimmie spoke. A native of Congo, she grew up speaking neither English nor Spanish, which are featured in the poem. "You are my other me," she said with a wide smile. Her classmates repeated her words. Students continued to speak, alternating languages as their classmates called back in chorus.

> "Si te hago daño a ti," "If I do harm to you,"
> "Me hago daño a mi mismo." "I do harm to myself."
> "Si te amo y respeto," "If I love and respect you,"
> "Me amo y respeto yo." "I love and respect myself."

Kimmie's teacher had introduced the poem as a ritual that began (and sometimes also ended) each class session. It served not only as a reliable launch to class but also reminded students that their work together wasn't typical schoolwork. The way they were together mattered, and one person's struggle could impact the entire group and vice versa. Kimmie, especially, cherished the ritual, becoming the de facto *In Lak'ech* leader for the class. When her class transitioned to online learning during the COVID-19 pandemic, Kimmie made sure they kept reciting the poem in the same cadence during video class meetings. While the poem has Mayan roots and is often leveraged in Indigenous Latine communities, we have increasingly observed it being taken up in diverse spaces. It's important to note that the poem is specifically Mayan, and as such, it is not universally accepted by all people within the Latine community. Be aware that using a ritual from a particular culture runs the risk of being colonizing, tokenistic, and othering. Who can and should use such rituals and in what contexts are important considerations.

We've also seen more culturally agnostic activities like *two truths and a lie* or *would you rather* be leveraged as recurring routines or rituals that ground youth and adults and bring them closer together. Consider setting check-ins, icebreakers, or reflections that can achieve similar aims. Think about ways that students can lead these recurring activities, similar to Kimmie's ownership of the poem routine.

GROUP AGREEMENTS AND DECISION-MAKING

Group agreements, as long as they are reinforced throughout a class's time together, are an essential resource for shifting responsibility for the class from the teacher to the community of learners. Students are accustomed to key decisions in class being made by the teacher. When a student breaks the rules, they look to the teacher to intervene. But what if you were able to develop a classroom community that developed group agreements to which everyone was accountable, including the teacher? Groups that do this shift the way power flows in the group, from reliance on the positional authority of the teacher to a set of ground rules that students have constructed.

Ben, one of this book's coauthors, saw a terrific example of this process while spending two years studying the evolution of a team of young people who conducted research at their high school in Oakland, California, through a program called Youth Engaged in Leadership and Learning (YELL).[5] One of the first decisions in YELL had to do with group ground rules for behavior. Youth defined unexcused absences, spelled out how many warnings students should receive for absences, specified the consequences of disrespecting others, and differentiated acceptable curses (directed toward oneself) from unacceptable curses (directed toward others). These deliberations, which the program director facilitated without giving input, took several afternoons. Some students found the whole exercise foreign. During a conversation at the beginning of the first year, one student said, in frustration at the slow pace, "I think y'all [the adults] should make the rules." Over time, however, the group agreements became a resource that allowed adults to deflect authority from themselves to a more impartial set of rules. As one youth participant, Marlene, said in an interview, "If we break the rules, we couldn't get mad because we were the ones that put them in force."

Young people gained a great deal of practice regulating their own work and behavior. Youth participants routinely initiated the meetings, explained the agenda, and helped keep the group on task. Every student facilitated a meeting at least once. In addition to facilitating group meetings, youth in YELL routinely worked in small teams with limited guidance from adults. Also, Ben observed occasions where a student reminded the program director if she had broken one of the group agreements. The director, mindful of the importance of accountability, reinforced this dynamic through her actions.

Aside from group agreements that guide the conduct of the classroom community, there will also be times when collective decisions must be made about how to proceed. This is most pivotal when it comes to selecting a topic, but group decisions also come into play when selecting research methods, deciding who to report findings to, and what kinds of calls to action to make. In advance of these decisions, it can help to develop and practice a decision-making protocol with your students.

The CCI curriculum includes two main decision-making protocols—democratic and consensus. In a common democratic approach, a class would list all the possible problems they would want to investigate. These lists are often quite long, filling a white board. The teacher then works with the students to combine or *bucket* similar problems. Then the students vote. We advise against winner-take-all at this phase because of the sheer volume of choices. Instead, conduct rounds of voting, eliminating the lowest vote-getters until you arrive at a small group of finalists—around three choices. Then hold a final vote where the winner takes all. This could be a vote with eyes closed, with slips of paper, or completely open, depending on the context.

While there are many consensus models, they all tend to be more time-consuming—but potentially more unifying than democratic votes. As we showed in the sidebar earlier in the chapter, in a true consensus model, all potential problems or choices are listed on the board, and then the class engages in discussions about each: Can you live with us choosing this? Can you support your peers in implementing it? Can you commit to this process to bring us closer together? Eliminate all options where students answer no to any of the questions above. When a small group of final choices are reached, score each one: 1) Love it; 2) Like it; 3) Meh; 4) No way. Use these ratings to drive a final discussion where (hopefully) clear consensus is reached.

WHAT TO AVOID AT THIS STAGE

- "Teacher-splaining," when teachers can't give up the idea that they actually know what is best for youth.
- Treating leadership as a reward rather than a learning opportunity.
- Being inconsistent in sticking to group agreements.

CONCLUSION

Key Takeaways

- Craft meaningful teacher-student partnerships by willingly sharing power with students.
- Make sure to walk to the walk of power-sharing approaches to deepen youth-adult partnerships.
- Build reciprocal trust as an important part of this process.
- Be vulnerable and real with students to increase your chances that trust is built.

Strategies from Teachers

- *Leadership roles.* Consider working with students to assign them key roles in the class or project. Roles could include facilitator, timekeeper, recorder, materials manager, survey designer, scheduler, field researcher, analyst, lead, liaison, or workflow coordinator.

- *Acts of vulnerability.* This is hard to prescribe, since it needs to be true to the context. In Nader's case, he shared a personal loss with great reward. The masks activity, where participants reflected on their inside and outside identities, and online icebreakers like scavenger hunts can help set a vulnerable stage. Accountability letters add personal weight to the work.
- *Community rituals.* The call-and-response poem worked well for the class in the chapter. Routinized check-ins, icebreakers, or reflections can achieve similar aims. Consider leveraging two pieces of our advice at once and have students lead these rituals.
- *Group agreements and decision-making.* Engage and support youth in creating their own rules for behavior. While it may be a difficult process, these rules are authentic to youth, and they are more likely to hold each other accountable because they created them.

Up Next: Elevating Students' Lived Experiences

Now that processes are in place for youth and adults to meaningfully build relationships, partner, share power, and trust each other, the conditions are ripe for exploring lived experiences as a way to begin examining social problems. We will share ideas and specific strategies for elevating the everyday to be an object of inquiry and action.

FIGURE 2.1 **Forming partnerships**

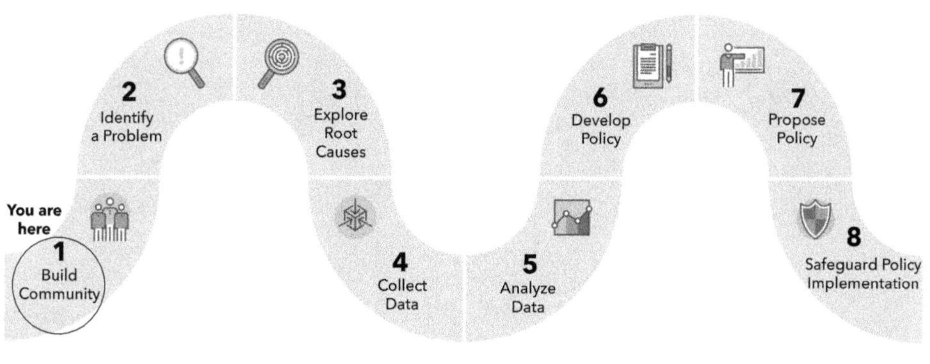

THREE

Elevating Students' Lived Experiences

IT'S AN ALL-STAFF PROFESSIONAL LEARNING DAY at Deerfield Regional School District, and the high school auditorium is full. All 140 of the teachers and administrators from the middle and high school sit in attendance. The opening session is a presentation from the student voice club, sharing the research they conducted during the past year. The audience gets quiet as the students take the stage. Their slides are queued up.

Raheem, a Black male sophomore who is one of the top football players, steps to the mic: "Instead of forcing me to cover parts of my body that aren't even sexual, maybe we should teach boys and men to be respectful," he says. The audience buzzes, confused about a masculine young man describing an issue that primarily affects young women.

Then Hank, a white male junior, speaks: "I've experienced discrimination in the classroom. Many teachers don't expect for African Americans to be in honors classes, so we're kind of singled out." The audience settles a bit, understanding the identity-bending motif the students are using.

Ebony, a Black female junior, says: "I've been called a 'spic,' been told to go back to my country."

Kara, a white female sophomore steps up: "I've been called a 'fag' often."

Angel, a Latine male junior, takes the mic and says, "Raise your hand if you have ever felt like someone treated you unfairly based on some part of your identity, like your race, ethnicity, gender, or anything else that makes you who you are? Well, that is what defines discrimination, and we have spent the last year exploring and researching how it affects students at Deerfield directly. Just like national data shows, statistically, students that deal with discrimination or bullying have lower grades, lower graduation rates, worse work ethics, and more."

You could have heard a pin drop in the auditorium at that moment. The students continued their presentation, sharing the data from their survey of over five hundred of their peers. The powerful element of this example, which we'll explore further in this chapter, is that the group of students were challenging business as usual at their school. Beyond sharing their varied experiences around the common problem of microaggressions and the lack of adult response, they created, with their teacher, a space and a process where they could share their lived experiences, be vulnerable, and support each other across their differences. This commitment to mutual support and safety led them to open their presentation with quotes—but for each student to read a quote that was obviously *not* from or about them.

While these student vignettes made for an entertaining and powerful presentation, their willingness to share and explore their own lived experiences was the foundation for their whole youth research project. When the young people shared about the problems they faced and listened to their peers do the same, classroom community and trust deepened. More importantly, the youth and their teacher kept the focus on the negative past experiences, using them as reminders about their important work together and motivation to take action against school-based oppression.

SOCIOPOLITICAL DEVELOPMENT

The most important part of Transformative Student Voice work is sociopolitical development for both young people *and* the adults who partner with them. Fundamental to that is the development of a *critical consciousness*, an understanding of how your identities interact with historical and institutional structures to result in privilege or marginalization. As you develop this understanding, you also develop skills to engage with other people in these conversations.

Lessons Learned

In prior work we explored the experiences of three teachers who engaged in these conversations over the course of a school year, and we learned a few key things.[1]

Get Comfortable with Discomfort

Adults must build their skills to engage students in talking about their lived experiences; these may touch on race, class, gender, and sexuality, as we explored in chapter 1. Most importantly, adults may need to get comfortable with discomfort. Sharing from personal experiences can be emotional and difficult. Solutions or fixes may not be immediately clear or tangible. This stage may involve students sitting with painful realities, such as the fact that their school is underachieving, their neighborhood is segregated, or city transit services don't meet their needs. This discomfort, though, can be an important part of the project. As students sit with and think through the injustices surrounding them, they can better understand themselves, the issues impacting them, and possible solutions.

Don't Give Up

Adults and young people have the difficult task of not giving up. They need to focus not on finding the right answer but on maintaining the drive to be curious, and possibly critical, about schools and society. They need to *not* give in to hopelessness and *not* accept "That's just the way it is" as an answer. Youth instead need to examine their lived experience as a catalyst for dreaming more just and equitable futures.

Build Relational Trust

Time must be spent building relational trust, sharing stories, and developing skills to ask questions and truly *hear* each other. We've observed many educators use a variation of the Vegas rule: what's said in the classroom stays in the classroom (unless the speaker gives permission for their story to be used in explicit ways, like a presentation hook or a quote for a policy proposal). This ensures that youth and adults can share freely and vulnerably about their experiences and feelings related to the problem they are researching.

STRATEGIES FOR CREATING SPACE

Below we share some specific strategies to get students talking about their lived experiences, both positive experiences that can be celebrated and bring the class closer together and negative experiences that could direct the group's future actions toward justice and equity.

"I Am" Poems

In our curriculum, one of the earliest activities meant to draw out students' lived experience involves "I Am" poems. Students see an example of the poem before writing their own using a series of sentence starters: *I am . . . I wonder . . . I see . . . I hear. . . .* Students are encouraged to reflect on their passions, communities, and interests, as well as on the issues they face. The depth of the poems often varies initially, as some students are more comfortable exploring themselves and sharing about their feelings, identities, and memories. Eventually, though, the poems are the first steps toward normalizing exploration of students' lived experience.

Returning to the opening vignette from the Deerfield students, their presentation hook deeply explored race, gender, and sexual orientation. While some youth are comfortable having conversations along those lines, many need support and scaffolding in sharing such personal and vulnerable details about themselves. While an "I Am" poem isn't the only way to get there, it has been successful for the teachers and students we support.

Problem Circles

In our curriculum, we suggest engaging in a *problem circle.* The process begins with students thinking about problems in their immediate lives, often school-based injustices. We position the activity as a way for students to locate themselves, their loved ones, and their experiences in the research they will be conducting. We ask why they care about the problem, how it has affected them, and general feelings about what's exciting, boring, or confusing about the issue. Youth reflect on those questions by writing, drawing, or just sitting silently.

Eventually, they begin to share. This can be done in pairs, small groups, or larger groups. The following chapter, on critical conversations, offers more thoughts and guidance on how to design and facilitate the discussion. Regardless of the structure, youth will likely share a variety of experiences—some may be light and funny, others perhaps heavy and emotional. All these answers have worth.

After everyone has shared, we ask a question we want the group to grapple with: *how does this problem affect you or people you care about?* Typically, students write their answers before sharing again. We add one last element in this round, however. After students have shared, we prompt them to do some initial qualitative analysis thinking by identifying any themes, patterns, or trends they heard from the discussion with their peers. This not only recaps the conversation—"It seems like this problem affects us in specific, shared ways"—but also begins to provide direction for our next steps.

Counternarratives

Adult narratives often dominate the framing of social problems. Think about gun rights, for example. The National Rifle Foundation and Moms Demand Action are two high-profile adult organizations that represent the poles of the argument. Emma González, who now goes by the first name X, changed the conversation during their speech at the March for Our Lives protest in Washington, DC, in March 2018. González shared about their experience surviving a shooting in Marjory Stoneman Douglas High School in Parkland, Florida.[2] Swedish climate activist Greta Thunberg achieved something similar in 2019 when she questioned world leaders at the United Nations Climate Action Summit. "How dare you?" she said with an intense scowl. "You have stolen my dreams and my childhood with your empty words."[3] These retorts from González and Thunberg against the dominant adult discourse represent *counternarratives*, a form of resistance literacy that has grown out of critical race theory.

Counternarratives challenge singular and often negative stories about young people, their identities, and their communities. The act of crafting and delivering a counternarrative, as González and Thunberg did, brings stories of lived experiences from the fringes of the debate to the center. Youth Participatory Action Research and TSV are counternarratives in their own right, emphasizing the experience and expertise of young people instead of adults.

While González's and Thunberg's counternarratives were highly publicized via conventional and social media, we've seen similar powerful examples emerge in classroom discussions and policy presentations to adults. At one high school, students held paper labels with hurtful comments they had heard from teachers written on them, including, "I'm poor," "I'm not smart enough for AP classes," and "You'll never amount to anything." After proposing a policy around cultural competence training for staff, the students declared they were more than their labels as they tore the papers in half. Each of the youth completed a sort of cycle of counternarrative during their presentation. They shared the adult point of view, in this case hurtful racist and classist assumptions about the young people's worth. Then, citing research they had conducted through peer interviews and surveys, the youth began to reclaim power over the issue. They asked their peers what they were feeling, what they did in response, what they were scared of, what they wanted to sustain, and what they wanted to interrupt. After analyzing the data and using it to drive policy demands, the students began to reframe the problem from student inferiority to teachers' lack of cultural competence. They brought it full circle by physically shredding the evidence of the adult point of view.

Lived Experience

Teachers often bemoan restrictive school structures, such as when curriculum is mandated with limited flexibility or adaptability. Nader, the teacher mentioned earlier, was forced to teach a scripted curriculum from a major curriculum developer. Instead of admitting defeat, he found ways to infuse as much of the TSV approach as he could, including humanizing practices and various dialogic strategies. After reading the classic middle school novel *Bud, Not Buddy,* about a ten-year-old Black boy searching for his biological father, Nader asked students to apply the central theme from the book (that hardships lead to transformations) to their own lives.[4] They used timelines and maps to explore when and where important or difficult things happened. They created clay models of themselves to better illustrate feelings and events. They wrote letters to their past and future selves, both exploring their hardships but also dreaming of transformative futures.

Not every educator will be able to do exactly what Nader did. The key, though, is that Nader found ways for the students to apply ideas from the book to their own lives. As it turned out, not only were their scores on the rigid standardized assessment strong, but Nader and the students had done something far more valuable: they had built trust and community that would eventually result in powerful youth research and action.

Discomfort

Returning to the idea of discomfort discussed earlier, it is imperative for teachers to understand themselves and be ready to mediate potentially heavy and serious information shared by students. How do you respond as a facilitator if someone shares a story of personal struggle, and no one responds? Do you sit in silence, move the conversation along, or do something else? An educator's stance matters. The fatal flaw for many folx is that they assume that there is a correct answer and that they must possess it. When it comes to listening to others' lived experience, that could get dangerous. While we will explore this in depth later in the book, we advocate taking a stance of not having the answer, but instead helping the youth find it. In the work of TSV, the adult's job is not naming problems and solely formulating solutions. Instead, adults should act more as facilitators, supporting young people in unpacking sometimes painful past or present experiences and eventually taking action to mediate them. Early in the process, that involves adults being good listeners.

Shelley often runs an activity where she gives participants a list of dream vacation spots (mountains, the beach, an urban oasis) and asks them to choose one. In pairs, people interview each other about why they made the choice they did, to discover what values led them to their decisions. In the second round, the participants are asked to persuade others to choose their selected vacation spot. In the first round, participants report feeling heard and listening with curiosity. In the second round, participants often report feeling more defensive, and the ensuing conversation tends to be more of a negotiation or debate. This activity has implications for educators. Listening out of curiosity is different from listening with an agenda. Youth tend to share more freely about themselves and their experiences in softer, more judgment-free spaces.

So, as an educator, do you feel a need to have an answer? Are you comfortable with there not being an answer? Can you find power in being a respectful witness to harm, trauma, or other emotions that young people share? It's important to know your comfort level, as well as ways to both mediate your own reaction and create a space where it is OK to share and explore feelings without having an answer.

Beyond your stance and the space you craft, it's good to have a few concrete strategies that allow you and the youth to find comfort in discomfort. Here are things to consider: Craft norms or ground rules that work for the context. A group of people who have never worked together will likely need different norms than a group that has been together for months. An assigned group will likely need to break the ice differently than one in which participants have chosen their group. Similarly, if folx are grouped by similarities or more mixed, the shared agreements and supports will likely need to be different as well.

GROUND RULE IDEAS

- *Vegas rule.* "What happens in this class, stays in this class" is generally a good way to allow safety for the person sharing and build a sense of trust.
- *Don't yuck my yum.* In the words of Ted Lasso, "Be curious, not judgmental." One person may like something the other doesn't. No need to judge, scold, or convince them differently.
- *Throw glitter, not shade.* Not only are we not judging, we are actively encouraging each other. When someone shares a tough memory or experience, glitter feels way better than shade.

Have a plan to deal with the gray if someone says something awkward. Some general strategies:

- *Permission to say "ouch!"* Empowering students to say "ouch!" when something hurts or is questionable can be an efficient and low-stakes way to express impact or disagreement in the moment. For example, if someone said, "I'm sick of all the basketball players always showing up late to class," a basketball player who is habitually punctual could say "ouch!" as a means of expressing their disagreement with the statement. Ideally, the speaker would amend their statement, keeping the conversation going as opposed to stopping it.
- *Stop, drop, and heal.* This is a fun way to not sweep things under the rug. As much as possible, craft a culture where people can be called in to discuss and mediate issues in the moment. As an educator, you can model this approach when something gets to you. In front of the class, stop the conversation, share your feelings, and engage with the classroom community to heal or attempt to find some sort of resolution.
- *Parking lot.* Have a space on a wall or poster where students can place sticky notes or write questions, concerns, ideas, or feelings. This is a place where issues can be noted and, eventually, addressed. This approach is best for topics that don't need immediate addressing. It is paramount to return to

these concerns, however, and it will require some planning or action steps. Unlike the "ouch!" approach, which surfaces concerns to be addressed immediately, the parking lot can often be forgotten. Create a schedule for checking and discussing parking lot issues.

TIPS FOR ELEVATING STUDENTS' LIVED EXPERIENCE

- Adults should consider sharing their lived experiences first to build trust and provide an example of how to do it.
- Allow lots of time to think, share, and process. This can be slow work.
- Anticipate problems, like students trying to find the perfect solution, enduring pressure from adults, and struggling to retain hope.

(For a variety of resources, visit TransformativeStudentVoice.net.)

WHAT TO AVOID AT THIS STAGE

- *Perfection.* This is still near the beginning of the process; we're still learning, not solving.
- *Pressure.* Adults can place unneeded pressure on the process. Some may try to pressure students to not hold the school or social systems accountable. Others may place too much value on the youth attaining a certain outcome. Neither is helpful.
- *Pessimism.* This is a hard process full of setbacks. As much as possible, try to keep a hopeful outlook.

CONCLUSION

Key Takeaways

- Students' lived experiences can fuel deep exploration of a problem and powerful social justice projects.
- Soliciting, sharing, and mediating those experiences should be done in a thoughtful, intentional way.
- Building trust, crafting safe avenues to share and discuss, and helping youth sit with their feelings and experiences can support the process.

Up Next: Critical Conversations

Now that students are beginning to consider and examine their own lived experiences, more critical conversations are on the way.

FIGURE 3.1 **Building trust**

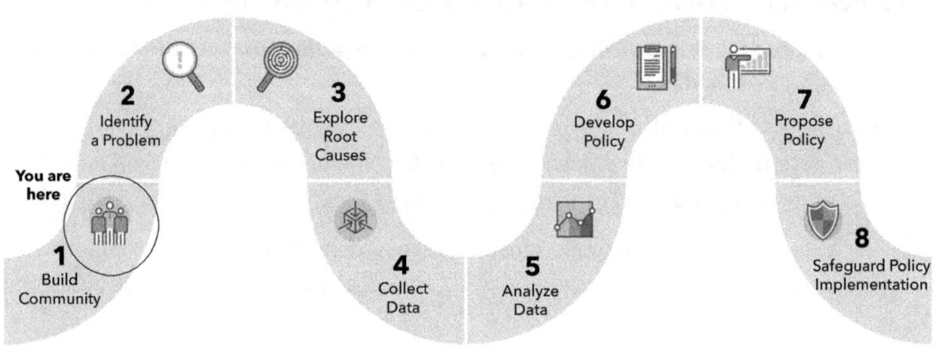

FOUR

Having Critical Conversations

THE ACTION CIVICS TEAM at John Lewis High School (JLHS) is known for being student run. The youth leaders plan the team's agenda and facilitate all meetings. While their adult coach attends all meetings, he takes a hands-off approach, believing that the team should be firmly student directed. The students know they can go to their coach when they need support, but they take pride in being student led. Though there are benefits to this approach, occasionally there are some challenges.

One year, when we were observing the work at JLHS, the team struggled to settle on the focus of their action civics project. The students in general agreed that the focus should be school safety, but which exact aspect of safety remained elusive. One of the youth leaders attempted to probe, asking questions about why students didn't feel safe in school and why there was a gang problem in their neighborhood. But the rest of the team, doing something we typically warn against, jumped to solutions. Students suggested that their policy might examine metal detectors, the use of clear backpacks, improving relationships between school staff and students, creating more community centers, and gang prevention programming. These young folx were smart and passionate, but they struggled to get a deeper understanding of the issue of school safety. Instead of conducting a root cause analysis, doing some initial research, or engaging in dialogue with each other about the conditions that have led to their school and community feeling unsafe, they jumped straight to a policy solution. To use a cliche, they put the cart (solutions) before the horse (research). If you look at the recurring graphic for our TSV cycle (at the end of every chapter), the youth, in this case, skipped almost half of the process.

The example of the JLHS students illustrates a key transition from the prior chapter, which emphasized the value of lived experience, to this chapter, which will emphasize critical consciousness. They overlap and inform each other but are not the same thing. Yes, to be consistent with chapter 3, we should design activities that invite and center the everyday knowledge and insights of young people. Yes, those most impacted by injustice—often students—bring unique insights about the contours, depth, and complexities of that injustice. But no, students do not come to the discussion of social problems as blank slates or burdened by "false consciousness."

Adults, you are not off the hook here. There is a role to play for a facilitator or educator who can ask good questions and challenge learners to reflect and analyze everyday realities in new ways. This is one of the trickiest and most nuanced distinctions when doing critical, anti-racist, or social justice work with young people. Educators, we at TSV included, often assume that awareness of the historic or systemic roots of inequality are self-evident to the young people experiencing that oppression. This awareness might come through everyday experience or family conversations for some, but it should not be assumed for all.

Educators can play key roles instigating or catalyzing reflection and discussion that stimulates critical consciousness. Digging into root causes and analyzing systemic factors is not necessarily a natural occurring phenomenon, especially in the United States, where dominant cultural models prioritize individuals as the locus of responsibility and agency. In our experience, critical analysis of root causes and systems benefits from scaffolded learning experiences and open conversation. For the youth at JLHS, they might have benefited from a challenge to their easy answers of metal detectors and clear backpacks, such as being asked to unpack what was at the root of their sense of the school not feeling safe. In this chapter, we will define critical consciousness, provide suggestions for fostering critical conversations in your classroom, address some things to avoid, and share a few examples of critical conversations in classrooms.

WHAT IS CRITICAL CONSCIOUSNESS?

Critical consciousness originated in the social and educational theories of the Brazilian educator Paulo Freire.[1] Freire developed his ideas through his work with rural adult farmers struggling with poverty and political marginalization. Through his culture circles and problem-posing approach, learners developed not only reading and writing skills but also a deep sense of agency as historical actors with the capacity to work as a collective for revolutionary change. They learned, in Freire's words, both the *word* and the *world.* As Freire noted, education can be a tool for integration or one for empowerment, participation, creativity, and connection. He certainly chose the latter and has been an inspiration to each of the authors in our journeys as scholars and activists.

Critical consciousness is central to Youth Participatory Action Research (YPAR); it is both a precursor to developing transformative projects and an outcome of those projects. Though we use the word *outcome*, we don't mean that it is static or finished. Critical consciousness is not a light switch that moves from off to on but is instead an ongoing, complicated process of inquiry, discovery, tension, and growth.

With students, we tend to prioritize two key ideas. First, to be critical means questioning common sense or "the way things are." It shifts from a passive view of social life—as inevitable or fated—to an exploration of the way we got here and a realization that there are alternatives. For example, take the idea of *meritocracy*, that those who get ahead do so based on their talents and effort. Meritocracy is a dominant narrative in the US, reinforced through media, films, and the speeches of elected officials on the left and the right. Critical conversations would invite us to ask questions about meritocracy and explore where it fails as an explanation of social hierarchies.

A second element to critical consciousness, which is closely related to questioning dominant narratives, is to recognize that our individual actions are embedded in a mix of institutional structures, cultural norms, and social relations. This is especially valuable for young people as they come to recognize that their own experiences are not isolated or unusual. Recognizing that personal experiences are shared by others diminishes feelings of stigma or isolation, directly challenging a "blame the victim" mentality. In chapter 7, we talk about a classroom of students aiming to address xenophobia toward Mexican

American students at their school. These students started by sharing personal essays about their own experiences, then exchanged their essays to read about each other's experiences. Students began to see that their own feelings—of being mistreated, of not belonging, of anger—were not just their own private or personal experience. Seeing their experience as *shared* fueled their motivation to act and also helped redirect the issue as a problem for the school to address.

Other skilled YPAR scholars have noted this process. Michelle Fine, for example, describes an encounter between youth from Tucson and New York City. After listening to a New York student describe his special education class, a Tucson youth observed, "Your special education is in the basement? Wow, all the way across the country, and ours is, too."[2] This kind or recognition of the interconnectedness of experiences can be quite powerful for young people who previously interpreted experiences of suffering or hardship as theirs alone.

This kind of educational work is challenging, even risky if not carried out in a way that is respectful of young people's dignity and agency. The point is not to persuade someone they are oppressed or deliver a lecture about how they should see the world. And even if the teachers feel ready to dive into a more question-oriented set of discussions, their students may not be. By the time they get to high school, students may have become accustomed to acting as passive learners. They may not have had any classroom experiences where they are asked to construct meaning where there is not one right answer. With these cautions in mind, we share tips for some initial tone-setting with critical conversations.

GETTING STARTED WITH CRITICAL CONVERSATIONS

Critical conversations call for intention and planning. We have been in some classrooms—as teachers and observers—where efforts to stimulate discussions about the topic fall flat. Maybe one particularly vocal student says something like, "Most students are just lazy," or "It's racist to talk about racial differences," which shuts down engagement from others. Maybe students think it's a waste of time to overcomplicate the issue and instead just want the teacher to tell them the answer. Moreover, current teacher demographics suggest that in many classrooms where students are Black, Latine, Asian American, or Indigenous, the teacher will be a white, middle-class woman. Teachers, including teachers of color, will vary from their students on many dimensions of identity and lived experiences. This separation or divide can create challenges for teachers and may also create greater discomfort or risk for students. Maybe students want to talk about the issue of racism and white supremacy but are reluctant out of fear of offending the teacher.

For these reasons, and more, we recommend intentional groundwork to create the conditions for multiple, overlapping, iterative conversations throughout the year. Step one is to name and invite critical conversations: *we're going to talk about the topic of racism in this class*. If your classroom hasn't already formulated group agreements that enable open and honest discussion, this is the time to do it. (See chapter 2 for tips on group agreements.)

In addition to the explicit invitation, modeling how to disagree can be useful at this time, too. Consider, if at all possible, inviting a colleague in to show what a respectful disagreement might look like around a controversial topic. In the rare occasions that we've been able to team teach with colleagues, we've found that these examples are engrossing for students and useful for showing that it can be done. If you can't invite a colleague, consider showing a brief video of people engaging in respectful and critical conversation. (Kid President's *How to Disagree* is a good example.[3]) Then ask students: what did you notice?

ACTIVITY SUGGESTIONS

Carlos, TSV team member

I like to use music, comic strips, and short stories to model critical conversations. Art is a safe starting point for this critical conversation. It is not so personal as to offend someone but also has room for rival interpretations that can feed dialogue. In this type of activity, I will have students read a short story (such as "The Ones Who Walked Away from Omelas" by Ursula K. Le Guin) out loud and ask for their impression of the piece.[4] These early discussions often remain superficial as students attempt to make a point that summarizes the entire story.

I will then engage the students in a line-by-line reading of the story. I might even use slides, for example, with the words of the story on the left and blank space on the right, where students can fill in their interpretations. To prompt students, I will ask them to consider the choice of words the author uses or how the imagery evoked in the story relates to their lived reality. Dialogue like this about a short story of six pages might last forty-five minutes to an hour. Slowly the students will begin to provide rival interpretations of lines and occasionally will challenge each other's thinking. Typically, students will be surprised that they spend so much time on a short story or the new depths of their understanding of the short story.

I usually end by asking students why they think we engaged in this activity. They will inevitably answer that this was about pushing their thinking and asking them to practice critical thought. I also tell them that this is a model for how I want them to engage in critical conversations during our time together.

Conversations About Structural Racism

Another possible starting point for critical conversations can come from having students reflect on their educational experience. Students raise all sorts of aspirations and concerns when given the opportunity to reflect on their educational experiences: better relationships with teachers, cleaner bathrooms, safer hallways, more ethnic studies classes. Sometimes, to get students thinking and talking about structural racism, teachers will direct the classroom gaze toward disparities in academic achievement, such as graduation rates, college-going rates, or test scores. Teachers do this because these statistics provide stark evidence of the problems in US schools, and they often spark important conversations in the class. The risk, however, is that without offering some sort of framework to make sense of these disparities—or without a really skilled facilitator—the questions can make some students in the classroom feel worse. Looking at disparities may be a crucial step in a YPAR project addressing structural or systemic racism, but we recommend starting first with a lesson on the *opportunity gap*, a term for the disparities in the kinds of opportunities available to students that tend to fall along lines of race, class, language, and citizenship status. It turns the gaze toward the social and institutional contexts available to learners, as opposed to treating their performance as if it were isolated from social context and solely the student's fault.

OPPORTUNITY GAP ACTIVITIES

- *Explore online resources as a class.* In the past decade, several rich online databases have been published that demonstrate vast disparities in opportunity across the US. Consider, for example, using the Opportunity Atlas website as a class to map different neighborhoods or towns in your state and see differences in access to college.[5] Other online resources include the *New York Times* database on college access, *ProPublica*'s Miseducation project, and the Education Trust.[6]

- *Visit neighboring schools.* Although it can be logistically challenging, the educational payoff is great. A science teacher we worked with at a school serving mostly children from low-income families set up a visit for her students to a neighboring school, which was just across the district boundary but was far better resourced. Simply walking around the building—seeing the library, gym, and other facilities—sparked a new appreciation of the opportunity gap.
- *Utilize photography.* Students at a second-chance school (for those who had been pushed out of conventional high schools), walked around their building and took pictures of the lunchroom, gym, and library. Taking pictures gave them some critical distance from what they might otherwise take for granted and also offered fuel for their subsequent presentations. By virtue of having attended more than one school, these students already had a critical appreciation, based on life experience, of the opportunity gap. Their teacher's wisdom came in facilitating opportunities for them to show it in their own way.

After engaging in opportunity gap activities, your students may want to dig into outcome data, such as graduate rates or achievement performance. This, too, may give them fuel for their specific action projects. But we think engaging in activities that prepare students for critical conversations must come first.

FACILITATING CRITICAL CONVERSATIONS

Like teaching, facilitating critical conversations is as much an art as a science. While there are some specific skills that will aid you in facilitating a critical conversation (see problem-posing education and the work of Freire), there are also some important dispositions to be considered. In this section we want to provide you with some tips on how to facilitate critical conversations, including developing your role as the facilitator, structuring your group, using critical questioning to problematize social conditions, and dealing with deficit perspectives.

Becoming a Facilitator

A good critical conversation facilitator keeps dialogue moving, engaging all participants and pushing the conversation deeper. As the facilitator, resist the temptation to insert yourself into or overly manage the direction of the discussion. In the role of facilitator, you are not expected to be an expert or to possess the "right" answer; instead, you want to encourage and model critical thinking to your students. Note that this is a departure from the role you might usually play as a teacher, so it might take practice. Basically, avoid lecturing and instead ask questions that get your students thinking about issues.

Another important consideration is to try to flatten hierarchy and reduce adultism in order to foster productive and equitable relationships with your youth. We encourage *broaching* with your students: specifically naming your identities and privileges, explaining to students how your identities might impact dialogue, and asking students how they feel about engaging in dialogue with you. By broaching at the outset of a critical conversation, you might model for students how you are attentive to power dynamics and are willing to engage in dialogue about difference.

ACTIVITY SUGGESTION

Carlos, TSV team member

Broaching is a concept more commonly discussed in multicultural counseling. The point of broaching is to provide the opportunity to address biases that exist in the room, naming these biases at the outset, and allowing them to be addressed rather than continue to fester in the background.

When I broach with a group of students I will say:

> I identify as a cisgender, heterosexual, Chicano male, of upper middle class. My identities likely differ from each of you in the room in some way. It might also be the first time some of you have been taught by a person with my identities. I am wondering how you might feel about these differences or if you have any reactions to me being your instructor?

Most often the group remains quiet for a few moments; the key here is not to fill the silence. Give the group time to reflect and answer even though it might feel uncomfortable. Classroom teachers often call this *wait time.* Some students will say that they have no concerns. Some students of color might even express excitement about working with a man of color. Occasionally, a student will admit to having some biases. A student once admitted to having trouble working with male authority figures; it was an issue we would have to check in on during our time working together. Even if no biases surface in this initial conversation, you have made the topic of difference one that is acceptable to address in the group.

Students might occasionally ask you questions directly, hoping you might provide a direct answer; in most cases it is wise to redirect these questions to the group. In cases like this, Carlos likes to say, "We are lucky to have a group of experts on the student experience in the room. Let's see what your classmates think!" By deferring to the other students in the room, you are setting up the expectations of a peer dialogue. In cases where the group is completely lost on the subject matter or the questions being asked, it might make sense to intercede and ask what the youth need to move the conversation forward.

Structuring Your Group

In critical conversations, group size is important. Famed liberation psychologist Maritza Montero observed that a group seeking to promote consciousness should be large enough to provide a diversity of opinion but small enough to encourage active engagement by all participants.[7] Though she did not specify a size, we think that a group of eight to twelve might be good for meeting these goals. If your group is larger, consider splitting into smaller groups. More senior group members might then take the facilitator roles, and you, the teacher, can roam between groups, providing suggestions and feedback to promote depth of thought.

We mentioned this above as it relates to the facilitator, but it bears repeating that the point of the group dialogue is peer-to-peer communication. Seek interaction and dialogue within the group that is peer based; regardless of class standing, identity, or experience, no group member is entitled to dominate the conversation or claim a position of superiority. One strategy to support this is to privilege the voice that has not spoken. If a student who has yet to speak raises their hand, they get priority over everyone else waiting to speak who has already spoken at least once. We've also seen *talking tokens* used to balance conversations. Every student gets two tokens. When they speak, they must place their token on the table. When they're out of tokens, they can't speak any further, creating space for other students to use their tokens and take part in the conversation.

Critical Questioning

The goal of critical conversations is to problematize dominant social narratives and increase awareness of the causes of current sociopolitical inequities. To this end, it is essential to raise questions about power differentials and why certain people are marginalized because of their nondominant identities. Antwi Akom emphasized that the facilitator must be explicit about sociopolitical inequities.[8] To this end, social inequities can be treated as a matter of fact; you might consider sharing graphics and statistics that highlight specific inequities. So don't debate the existence of the wage gap between men and women; instead push your students to consider the *why* behind these inequities.

Because so much of our daily experience goes unquestioned, people seldom consider why sociopolitical inequities exist. Worse yet, many buy into dominant discourse that rationalizes inequities—unemployment is high because people are lazy, or immigrants steal jobs. As the facilitator, your job is to question this assumed "normal." In challenging dominant narratives, ask youth to reflect on their personal experiences. We have observed that often people can be quick to judge abstract others (whether other students or other communities) but apply more nuanced judgments of themselves. Ask them: Do you see yourselves as being lazy? Do you see family members who have to work multiple jobs to make ends meet? Questions like these, anchored in lived experience, start to chip away at dominant narratives and provide space for counternarratives, which we discussed in depth in the previous chapter. Students begin to engage with the reasons behind the narrative. For example, you might ask students: who benefits from a narrative that unemployment is high because younger generations are lazy?

Often it is easiest to start critical conversations and social analysis through the lens of the media. Roderick Watts describes the use of hip-hop music and music videos as a means for raising consciousness in Black boys. After watching a video, for example, he would engage the youth with five questions: "What did you see? What does it mean? Why do you think that? How do you think and feel about what you saw and heard? What would you do to make it better?"[9] These five questions could easily be adapted to any critical conversation. In a classroom, we might place these five questions on a poster board and hang them in a position of prominence, so students can refer to them during a dialogue. We find the question *Why do you think that?* particularly useful, as it calls on students to provide evidence or think more critically about their response.

Challenging Deficit Narratives

Occasionally in a critical conversation you will come across a student or group of students who endorse a deficit perspective. In a recent student voice workshop, for example, Carlos interacted with students who felt that youth should not serve on teacher hiring committees because kids would just pick teachers who were easy—not actually interested in teaching but willing to let students do their own thing. In this example, it was important for Carlos to gently push the youth on their thinking. Why did they think students would behave this way? Would the students espousing this belief behave this way themselves? There was a bit of discussion about how these ideas stemmed from adultist beliefs that kids can't be trusted with important decisions. Another group of students challenged this line of thinking, saying they felt students would be great on hiring committees, since students know the qualities of good teachers. Young people also affirmed that it was important to find out if a teacher candidate could understand the cultural backgrounds of the students.

In challenging deficit perspectives, it is important not to shame or make the student defensive. Either of these reactions halts discussions. Instead, ask questions that help the student clarify their position and the rationale for their position. As with Carlos' example, ask the student if the perspective they are espousing is something that is true for them personally. Ask the student to provide support for their position, specific examples of when they have seen such a thing happen. As a facilitator, your job is to encourage questions, not to instruct youth on the right answer. So in cases of deficit perspectives, we ask questions to provoke thought and help the students draw their own conclusions.

WHAT TO AVOID AT THIS STAGE

- Looking for one right answer. Be curious, think things through, and don't force a solution to the issues students are bringing up.
- Valuing vocabulary more than meaning-making. Worry more about critical thinking than vocabulary. Thinking about the patriarchy is more important than using the word correctly.
- Telling students how to think or what words to use.
- Shrinking from difficult conversations or questions.

(For more ideas, visit TransformativeStudentVoice.net.)

CONCLUSION

Key Takeaways

- Critical consciousness is not a light switch that moves from off to on, but instead an ongoing, complicated process of inquiry, discovery, tension, and growth.
- Name and invite critical conversations: *Today we are talking about racism.*
- Music, video, and art can be nice segues into critical conversations.
- The facilitator and group structure play important parts in critical conversations.

Up Next: Selecting a Topic

All of the critical consciousness work in this chapter wasn't merely a thinking exercise; it's all in service of the next chapter and the first major milestone in the CCI process: selecting a focal topic or problem.

FIGURE 4.1 **Having critical conversations**

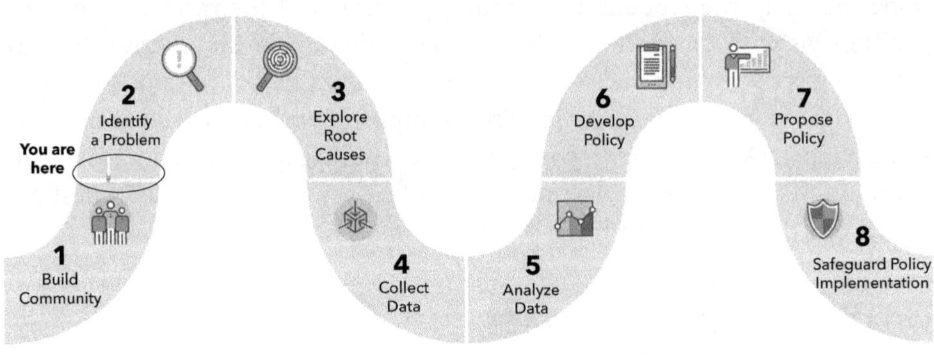

FIVE

Selecting a Topic

A STUDENT FROM PLAINS VIEW HIGH SCHOOL, a large, comprehensive high school, stood with her classmates on a stage and asked a packed audience to fill in the blank: "The wheels on the bus go . . ." she said, pausing for the audience.

"Round and round," the audience loudly responded.

"Uh, not at Plains View they don't," the student sassily said as the audience laughed.

Another student took the mic: "We identified transportation as our biggest equity issue at Plains View High School." She described how the city bus system doesn't serve the school; students must walk roughly thirty minutes from the nearest bus stop. This resulted in mass tardies. She explained how the students were at first looking at the tardies themselves as the problem. After conducting root cause analysis (which we will explain further in the following chapter) and meeting with adult partners, the young people began to see that student lateness was a symptom of a broader issue. Tardies were merely an indication; ensuring students had safe, efficient, and reliable transportation options to get to school was what really interested and motivated the youth.

This transportation problem was ideal for Youth Participatory Action Research. The topic was easily identifiable as a social justice issue, proved interesting and complex enough to keep students engaged, affected many students directly, and provided opportunities to connect with adult and community allies. Not all nineteen students in the class faced these exact transportation challenges. Some got rides from their parents or had cars themselves. Some lived close enough to walk. All, however, easily saw how transportation to and from school was an equity or social justice issue even if they had trouble articulating it at this early stage. They could see that some students had long and difficult trips because they lacked access to cars or direct bus routes. For students who could access cars or lived in neighborhoods with better transit options, the trip to school was quick and easy by comparison. This motivated the class to tackle the problem even when it got confusing or boring. Through activities meant to elevate youths' lived experience and develop critical consciousness, like those we mentioned in the previous two chapters, several students in the class had shared openly and emotionally about their struggles to get to school on time. This allowed the students who didn't face similar efforts to understand the problem and develop empathy for their peers. The complexity of the problem, and its public nature, also naturally drove students to connect with elected officials and school district personnel.

While the Plains View students eventually landed on what we saw as an excellent problem to research, it's not always so easy. In this chapter we share guidance, examples, and pitfalls related to problem selection in the Critical Civic Inquiry (CCI) process.

CHOOSING THE PROBLEM

While every part of the CCI cycle is important, settling on a problem that is engaging and motivating for students, while also allowing for deep and meaningful research, is one of the most pivotal. We've been doing this work in classrooms for fifteen years, and we've learned *a lot* about what focal problems tend to work best for this kind of youth-driven inquiry. (We also often call these *topics* or *issues.*) A bad example: plastics in the ocean. While this is an important topic, this problem is literally far away from the students, and their impact is more indirect. A better example: the transportation issue. This topic is literally close to the youth, it affects them and people they care about (their classmates and friends), and they can—and did, in this case—make a direct impact on the problem.

CHOOSING A GOOD FOCAL PROBLEM

Does the problem:

- *affect you or someone you care about?* Good problems are *near and dear* to the student, both emotionally and in terms of proximity. That means the problem likely impacts them, someone important in their lives, or both.
- *address a social justice issue?* Good problems tend to connect to inequitable access to resources or opportunities and apply to a broader policy or social context.
- *have the potential to bring in allies?* Good problems allow for community organizing within the school, in the broader community, and even with elected officials.
- *fire you up enough to persist through setbacks?* Good problems are interesting and complex enough to support sustained equity. As Carlos often reminds students, they will be working on this project for the better part of a year, and some students haven't had romantic relationships that have lasted that long.

And finally,

- *Can the teacher support the students in this investigation?* Good problems tend to walk a critical line, but in a way that doesn't risk students facing heavy discipline or educators losing their jobs. It's a difficult task for adults to support what can be seen as radical youth movements, but the right problem can allow for important, appropriate youth-adult partnerships.

Giving Guidance

So how do you get youth to agree on one problem that meets all these criteria? It certainly isn't easy. The first step is making sure you haven't skipped all the stuff we've covered before. Choosing a good problem grows out of spaces with self-aware educators who have built trust with students and engaged in critical conversations about young people's lived experience with social issues.

At this stage, we especially like to utilize an activity called *our dream school.* When Dane taught middle school writing, he first set up this assignment as an act in observation and descriptive writing, asking students to record their journey to school, experience at school, and return trip home. The students turned in assignments that seemed to glorify both the school and its surroundings, mentioning things like the size of the building, clean bathrooms, and new(ish) technology. While the youth did flex some nice descriptive writing skills, Dane feared they'd missed the point. In noting all the positive comments, he remarked in front of the class, "Wow, that must mean this school is perfect then." The youth quickly perked up: "Well, lunch could be better . . . And these uniforms are kind of restrictive . . . And the teachers are almost all white . . . And school starts too early."

This proved a perfect segue into the second phase of the dream school project: audaciously dreaming of a school built on students' terms. While this school will likely never be fully realized, the dreams students put forth inform both the problems they want to investigate and, eventually, possible solutions. We've heard wild ideas—gold-plated toilet seats, cloning favorite teachers, having a permanent fried chicken station in the cafeteria. But we've seen this activity raise important issues that pave the way for powerful youth research and policy building. Some of these dreams have included wishing for inclusive curricula, culturally relevant educators, and police-free schools. While a clear research problem may not always emerge, the dream school activity at least positions students to share about their current, likely imperfect experiences at school while dreaming of more just and inclusive policies. This also connects to critical thinking, which we covered deeply in chapter 3, and the ability to think beyond marginalization.

We next recommend transitioning to a related broad question: what does our community need to work on? This could be set up with a think-write-pair-share activity, where students consider the question, jot a response, find a partner, and engage in conversation. Eventually, the conversations could snowball into a whole-group discussion where ideas are shared and recorded. At this stage, we recommend vetting the problems with a series of questions (see the *Choosing a Good Focal Problem* sidebar earlier). This could lead to combining or eliminating problems. For example, *tardies* and *transportation* could be combined into one problem, as the Plains View students showed in the intro to this chapter. You may also need to cut problems (like plastics in the ocean) that don't meet our criteria. Finally, leverage group decision-making protocols to select the focal problem(s).

Note the plural choice for problems. Issue selection forces a pivotal decision in the CCI process. Will the entire class focus on one specific problem?

This is typically how CCI projects are done, but it certainly isn't the only way. You could divide the class into small groups with each investigating a different problem of interest. It may even be possible to allow each individual student in the class to choose their own topic. The more the group is fragmented, however, the heavier the lift tends to be on the educator. In this approach, as we've noted, adults and youth partner together. How realistic is it for one adult to meaningfully partner with four groups, eight, thirty? Finding articles and other resources and supporting complex conversations is likely challenging enough. It can be done, certainly, but your context should drive such major decisions.

Group Decision-Making

A key challenge with topic selection, beyond meeting the criteria we've already shared, is making decisions as a group, especially if students cannot come to agreement about the problem they want to tackle. Typically, this involves a laundry list of issues written on a white board. Some problems are crossed out. Others have arrows connecting to similar ideas. One group of students seem to be coalescing around a specific idea, while another appears to support something else. It can be difficult to find clarity in the chaos.

In our CCI curriculum, we treat group decision-making as an important skill to learn and practice. To provide a conceptual scaffold, we distinguish between four decision-making processes (as shown in the sidebar). We recommend that educators avoid *autocratic* and *representative* protocols, as those tend to limit the number of students involved. In the spirit of TSV, *democratic* and *consensus* approaches are better fits. While finding consensus is difficult, we encourage you to give it a try. The goal is to engage all students in the topic selection discussion and eventually land on an issue that everyone can at least tolerate. We hope all students can commit to supporting their peers in exploring the problem *and* contributing to its eventual solution. Eliminate topics where students can't make these commitments. Discuss. Negotiate. Revise the problem focus. If, eventually, the process falters, you have a few options. As explored earlier, you could have two or more groups focusing on different topics. Or you could abandon the consensus model and pivot to a democratic vote to break any deadlocks.

GROUP DECISION-MAKING PROCESSES

- *Autocratic.* A leader is selected (via voting, appointment, chance, etc.). After hearing proposals from various groups or individuals, the autocrat makes the final decision.
- *Representative.* The class chooses one or more representatives who make the final decision. Representatives are encouraged to gauge constituent interest before voting.
- *Democratic.* One or more rounds of voting are used to select the focal problem. This can be done anonymously (written votes or heads down, hands up) or in completely public ways (raising hands, moving to a corner of the room, dot voting).
- *Consensus.* A decision is made with an attempt to ensure everyone's buy-in. Helpful guiding questions include: Can you live with us choosing this problem? Can you support your peers in researching it? Can you commit to being part of this problem's solution? Revisions or negotiations may be needed to arrive at the final focal problem.

Examples

So what does this look and feel like in a classroom? Anastasia, a student at Plains View, remembers that she and her classmates considered the question: what does our community need to work on? The topic of truancies quickly emerged. Anastasia remembers students saying, "Kids aren't showing up to class," and "We really could do better as a school at that." They then considered counter-narratives. Teachers and administrators seemed to be implying that the truancies were solely the fault of the students. While that initially made sense, Anastasia began to feel that it was too simplistic and, frankly, offensive. She felt like adults were implying that the students were lazy or just prone to being late. As the class discussion progressed, students began sharing more about their own experiences, revealing that neither the district nor the city offered transit services to the school from one of its major feeder neighborhoods.

Anastasia was excited and ready to move forward with the transportation project. Some of her classmates, though, were dubious: *roads? routes? buses?—that sounds boring.* Those students thought examining mental health issues in the school sounded more interesting. Instead of forcing a choice in that moment, Anastasia's teacher let the process play out over time, positioning the students to explore both problems a bit more deeply before selecting just one. Part of that exploration connected the youth with an elected transit official representing their region of the city. The official framed transportation inequity as an umbrella problem. Dangling from that umbrella were several other intersectional problems including educational inequity. That's when it clicked for Anastasia and many of her classmates: if you can't access transportation, you can't make it to school on time, and your experience of school and maybe even achievement will be negatively impacted. With that new framing in place, the students found consensus around transportation as their focal issue.

While Anastasia and her classmates engaged in one successful way to do this, we've seen students and educators select focal problems in vastly different ways. In one example, an underenrolled public high school had been divided into two charter schools. The students at both schools identified fractured culture on the campus as a major problem. Initially, they committed a grave CCI mistake, jumping to a solution before fully understanding their problem, and proposed developing a social media app to bridge the gap. It turned out that the youth had perhaps initially focused on the wrong problem altogether. Three years later, their focus had shifted, and they worked with the school board to achieve something huge: reunifying the two charter schools into one public school. Even though the young people initially got sidelined by false solutions, the youth had isolated a strong problem and eventually developed real and powerful policies to address it.

Sometimes identifying a focal problem can be hard. A district-run student voice team, which brought together Black and Brown youth from across the district, experienced such a struggle. They had engaged in several activities designed to help them select a topic but were unable to come to any agreement. Some students, for example, advocated for better teachers, while others wanted the team to focus on implementing an ethnic studies curriculum. Fortunately, an adult partner helped the youth to take a step back. This partner encouraged the youth to return to the dream school activity they had previously completed. The young people looked for themes across their dream schools. They also looked for themes across the various issues they were debating. What they realized was that their dream schools and topics of interest were all in some way related to cultural representation. These Black and Brown youth desired more cultural validation in their educational experience, wanting to see themselves represented in positive ways in the curriculum and in district faculty and staff. Ultimately, the students decided to focus on district standards that would require the inclusion of diversity across subject areas, the inclusion of an ethnic studies requirement, and increasing faculty and staff diversity.

Pitfalls

There are several things to avoid when engaging in problem selection. It's best to avoid jumping to solutions before fully understanding and researching the problem. If youth have immediate good ideas, awesome! Develop a parking lot or some other dedicated space and system for questions to record them to return to later. Trying to find the *right* answer or *perfect* solution can be a trap. Problems can have several solutions, many of them dependent on context, such as the school's culture or the students' identities. As much as possible, be patient and allow the ensuing steps of root cause analysis (chapter 6), youth-led research (chapter 7), and data analysis (chapters 8 and 9) to organically reveal policy solutions in response to students' lived experience of the problem. The more they can explore the problem and be open to emergent insights with their peers, the better. We often see youth jump straight to a solution or answer without letting the research process play out. Many times, that's unfortunate, as this approach can block off creative or unexpected directions for the work. There will be plenty of time for exploration and creation of a policy solution at the end of the process. For now, students are ideally deepening their understanding of the problem and the way it has affected their lives or experience of school.

Adults should, as much as possible, support youth in selecting a problem as opposed to choosing one themselves. You may be stoked about a certain problem or itching to propose a certain solution, but, as an adult, it's not about you. We at TSV would rather see youth select their own problem and struggle as opposed to being force-fed an issue by an adult and more easily navigate the CCI cycle. Similarly, teachers should be honest if they feel they can't support a problem. They may not have the knowledge or skills to be helpful, or they may even be opposed to what the students are trying to achieve.

You should obviously heed *all* our earlier advice about selecting good problems, but let us again stress the importance of *proximity* and *urgency* in problem selection. The problem should be close to the youth. This means the problem should be immediately living around them—like transportation issues making students tardy, the effects of a splintered school, feelings of exclusion at their school, or political barriers for undocumented students. And it should also have a close impact either on the students themselves or on people they care about. This is where problems that are far away, abstract, or not prevalent in youth's lives tend to not be as successful. Students can't easily see and feel the effects of those issues. We're not saying the topics themselves are unimportant; they are very important. They just don't lend themselves as well to CCI.

CONCLUSION

Key Takeaways

- Problem selection is one of the most important parts of the process, and it connects to several key decisions and pitfalls.
- Finding consensus, as much as possible, is a strong approach for selecting a problem.
- Focusing on more than one problem within a class is possible, but it presents challenges for educators.
- Avoid settling on solutions at this point; fully explore the problem first.

Up Next: Root Cause Analysis

Take a second and celebrate. You've chosen a problem and completed the second phase of the CCI cycle. That's a huge part of the process. As we advised, it's now time to deeply explore the issue. That starts with a root cause analysis and, brace yourself, there are babies in the river.

FIGURE 5.1 **Choosing an Issue**

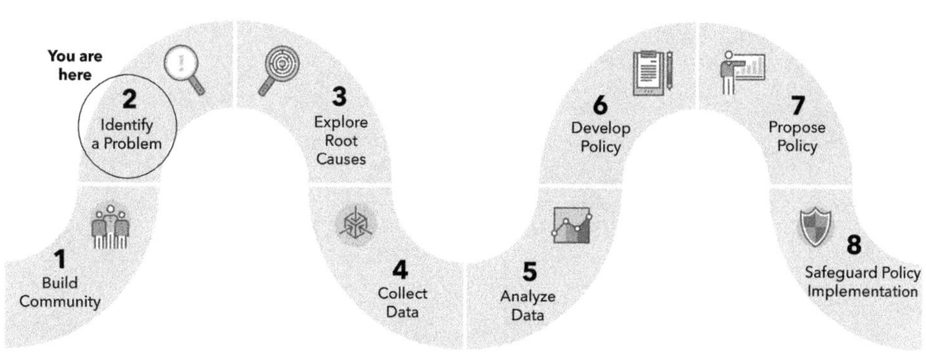

SECTION THREE

Critical Inquiry in Groups

WE FOLLOW A MODEL THAT BEGINS with the self and moves outward. Students begin by reflecting on their own experiences with the issue—how it has affected them, what they know about it, and what questions they have. Once students have named their own experiences, they are ready to engage in systematic inquiry about a broader sample of their school or community. This section takes teachers through this process, including deciding what kinds of methods to use, how to keep track of data (and not collect too much!), and various methods for analyzing data. We've designed this section to be relevant for multiple subject areas, including math, literacy, science, and social studies. The section's "traps" identify challenges associated with making sense of data.

SIX

Root Cause Analysis

IMAGINE WALKING DOWN A RIVER with a friend. It's a beautiful early summer day with sunshine glinting off the swiftly moving water. Something catches your eye, something bobbing in the water.

"Is that a baby?!?" your friend says in distress.

You squint your eyes. With shock and horror, you realize that it is in fact an infant floating in the water. Then you see another. And another. And even more. Babies bob as far upriver as you can see.

You hear a splash. Your friend has jumped into the river, grabbing one baby and another. Several babies float past your friend's grasp, as you sprint up the river.

"Where are you going?!?" your friend asks, surprised you're not helping.

"I'm going to stop whoever is throwing the babies in the river." You run as fast as you can.

This parable above is often used in community organizing workshops.[1] It sparks terrific conversations about how to intervene to address problems. We generally call this *root cause analysis*. This chapter mixes classroom-based evidence with actionable activities and aims to help youth researchers distinguish symptoms (the babies) from the root cause (the thrower). We also discuss the reality that some symptoms may need immediate attention before the root cause can be addressed.

FROM INDIVIDUALS TO SYSTEMS

As we mentioned in the previous chapter, selecting a problem can be difficult; exploring and truly understanding it can be even harder. Root cause analysis is crucial in student voice work. When youth can identify and address the root causes of problems, their advocacy is likely to be more successful in addressing their identified problem. Systems tend to implicate individuals instead of themselves. In schools, this looks like adults—administrators, teachers, staff—often blaming students either explicitly through punishments or implicitly through testing and other labeling: *They're late because they're lazy. They don't achieve because they can't read on grade level.* While some of these individualized contexts may require more exploration, blaming the individual is too easy an answer. We push students and educators to reject these deficit narratives about individuals and instead engage in exploration of the role school and social systems play in inequity.

The Root in Root Cause

The river parable isn't our only go-to method. We also love *root cause trees*. In fact, we're willing to bet that if you come to a TSV event in Colorado, New Jersey, Wisconsin, or any of our other growing partner sites across the country, you're going to see at least one youth team display a root cause tree. (To be fair, you'll also hear the river parable a few times as well.) A root cause tree breaks the problem into four main categories: The trunk represents the problem itself. The leaves are symptoms of the problem. The limbs are metaphors for factors, experiences, or situations that lead to those symptoms. The roots, quite literally, are the root causes of the problem. These causes often include policies, events, and societal choices that have resulted in inequitable opportunities or resource distribution for certain groups of people.

ROOT CAUSE TREE

The parts of the root cause tree:

- *Trunk (problem).* What is the focal problem?
- *Leaves (symptoms).* How do they show up in young people's lives? What emotions or feelings occur?

FIGURE 6.1 **Root cause tree**

- *Limbs (factors).* What settings, situations, or other contexts lead to your feeling these symptoms? What allows the problem to reach and affect you?
- *Roots (events or policies).* What are the social, political, and historical origins of the problem? What choices have been made that led to this?

The Plains View students shared a root cause tree in their transportation presentation. They named transportation as the trunk, or main problem. They listed punishments, poor grades, stress, and lack of sleep as symptoms, or leaves. The tardies and the process surrounding them were the limbs, or situations connecting the problem to the symptoms. The roots included things like distance from school, lack of public bus routes, lack of school bus drivers, and dwindling funding and ridership for mass transit coming out of the COVID-19 pandemic. The students also named race-based segregation as a root cause. The main issue was that the school lacked a bus connection to a certain feeder neighborhood, which happened to be traditionally underserved and consisted of mostly Black and Latine residents. In other words, the students felt like the lack of a bus connection served as yet another disappointing example of the city not serving their neighborhood. This exercise, then, helped the students not only push toward a systems framing of the problem, but it allowed them to deepen their understanding of the issue while also raising further complex and complicated questions.

EXPERT ADVICE

In writing this chapter, we asked a group of seasoned adult facilitators to share their favorite root cause activities or approaches. Here's what they shared:

- *Ladder of inference.* The ladder metaphor helps describe the problem while acknowledging the sometimes harmful role inference can play. Toward the beginning of the conversation, youth and adults engage in fact-based descriptions of the problem. As they move up the ladder, they attach more inferences, which lead to findings or conclusions. This *just the facts* start keeps the initial focus on observations or experiences, which is important.
- *Common cold.* Like the tree, the cold framing focuses on symptoms or root causes. When you're sick and have a cold, the symptoms may look like coughing, sneezing, and a runny nose. What, though, caused the problem? Things like stress, lack of sleep, poor nutrition, and other conditions could be at play.
- *Smoking mirror.* Our partners in a Colorado public school system leverage the Aztec cosmological framework of Nahui Ollin in tandem with TSV practices.[2] The Aztec deity Tezcatlipoca is used to frame self-reflection as a smoking mirror. The smoke represents socialization and norms that sometimes cloud the truth. One must move the smoke around to dig deeper and conduct analysis that reveals the root cause.

- *History and positionality.* Like the tree, this approach inspired by ethnic studies starts with the symptoms, but it then engages in historical and identity analysis. What are the historical roots of the problem? How does it manifest in contemporary society? Who is being served and in what ways? Who isn't? What is being sustained or interrupted over time?

SAVING THE BABIES

As we mentioned before, we realize that some symptoms may need immediate attention before the root cause can be addressed. In earlier chapters, we mentioned an ESL teacher, Mark. He worked with students to better understand and change racist demonstrations around Cinco de Mayo at their school. We would argue that the demonstrations were a symptom of greater race- and identity-based oppression in the school, but they were so hurtful and egregious that they couldn't be left to simply float down the river. A strict subscriber to pure root cause analysis might critique the youth for dwelling too long on the symptoms and not enough on the root cause. We are not so judgmental. We understand that the racist demonstrations likely had big impacts on the students and even their teacher. While a more inviting school culture may have been the goal on a holistic level, Mark and his students felt these hurtful events first needed to be redressed in the moment. Failing to address these concerns might be akin to brushing off their significance, which could be even more painful than the original event. Additionally, failing to process raw emotions might allow them to reemerge later in inopportune moments. For example, a student with pent-up frustrations might call out a school leader for being racist, which could damage opportunity for collaboration. We respect that, while also hoping the students don't dwell too long in the hurt. We want them to sit with it and fully understand and process their feelings, but we also want that pain to be in service of something generative, pushing them to deepen their research and eventually take action in response to the root causes.

EDUCATOR EXAMPLES

Often the economics of the housing market make gentrification seem like "it's just the way of the market." In one high school civics class, the teacher used the

CCI approach to encourage students to dig beyond simple answers as they explored the problem of gentrification in their neighborhood. One student's abuela became the class's guru, in some ways. The students and teacher turned to the older woman as a sort of guide through history, describing how the neighborhood had changed, first through waves of immigration and then because of rising property values. The students bounced their ideas off her and often invited her to class either in person or remotely. Her lived experience gave historical roots and personal weight to the problem. She also served as a model or example of how to talk about memories and experiences in meaningful ways and to reject statements like, "It's just the way it is." The students then began investigating how state and local policies affected the supply and price of housing.

In another high school, young women shared challenges with accessing feminine hygiene products. The school turned a mostly deaf ear, telling the students it was a personal problem. In other words, the school positioned the students as the problem. The young women rejected this framing and, instead, kept sharing their stories. One student shared that she was scared to bring up the topic with her conservative parents. Others told stories about accidents or apprehension that made learning almost impossible as their health needs went unmet, even citing Maslow's hierarchy of needs in their arguments.[3] Free products, the young women decided, were the solution to this root cause problem of access and availability. Eventually, the young women worked with Planned Parenthood to stock free menstruation products (as well as information about safe sex practices) in school bathrooms. This partially addressed the root cause in an important way by providing the young women the products they needed in the moment. The students readily admitted that they still had work to do when it came to gaining understanding and support from their families and school administrators.

Root cause analysis often doesn't go smoothly. When a group of high schoolers noticed an increase in fights and arguments between students, they wanted to know what was causing it. Initially, they considered that maybe something was wrong with the students, like they had lost their ability to get along while sequestered during the COVID-19 pandemic. Or maybe the culprit was behavior management; the teachers and admin had become too lax, and the students were taking advantage of it. Either way, the fights needed to stop. The students began conducting research, talking to their peers. They began to hear something that brought their two ideas together into a new hypothesis. Nothing was *wrong* with the youth, their peers reported; they just didn't have the relational skills they wished they had. Related to that, the teachers had lowered the bar on curriculum as opposed to behavior management. The students in the school wanted their learning in classes to be useful in their lives. Instead of archaic health classes, the students wanted current and dynamic comprehensive health classes that focused on healthy relationships (both in friendship and romance). Instead of staid labeling and memory recall questions about the human body, the students wanted to better understand their mental health, including coping and de-escalation strategies.

The youth researchers did something both smart and hard at this juncture. They listened to their research and changed course. They returned to their root cause analysis, realized it was off base, and revised the entire project. That meant conducting more root cause analysis, more research, more tough conversations within the team. While this research is still ongoing, the youth have switched from blaming students or teachers to demanding to work with administration to revamp the health and advisement curricula to focus more on healthy relationships and mental health strategies. While the problem is rigorous, the youth researchers' complex analysis and willingness to change course appear to be leading them toward an actionable solution.

What happens if students get stuck on thinking a symptom is the root cause? Two previous chapters can be especially helpful with root cause facilitation. In chapter 3, we shared the idea of counternarratives, and in chapter 4, we shared strategies for facilitating difficult conversations. If students, for example, are adamant that youth laziness is the root cause for a school problem, ask them to reflect on times where they personally were or weren't lazy. Then, perhaps, engage them in writing a counternarrative to the assumption that students are lazy.

WHAT TO AVOID AT THIS STAGE

- *Cutting corners.* We've stressed this several times in the book, but it's worth repeating. Don't rush the process, jump to the solution, or take shortcuts. The struggle to find the root cause is a generative pursuit.
- *Getting locked on the root.* While it definitely is best not to get bogged down fighting symptoms of the problem, some issues may require mediating pain in the moment. It's

OK to (as we said in chapter 3) *stop, drop, and heal*. When appropriate, though, start attacking that root cause again.

- *Giving up*. We've seen many teams struggle at this stage as the rigor of real-life problems gets more difficult. Confusion, tears, and arguments are all common at this phase. While that dissonance can be helpful, be sure to leverage other fun, communal activities to bring some levity to the heavy conversations.

CONCLUSION

Key Takeaways

- Root cause analysis is an important part of the TSV process, as it pushes past easy, convenient, or just plain wrong assumptions and directs student efforts toward the true or biggest cause of the problem.
- Metaphors are helpful. We've mentioned rivers, trees, ladders, colds, smoke, and intersections as frames that can support youth in root cause analysis.
- Be flexible, as the root cause analysis may drastically shift what youth thought they were initially doing. In other words, don't be afraid to revise your project based on new learnings.

Up Next: Collecting Data

Now that you've selected an important problem and have engaged in root cause analysis, it is now time to gather data about the problem and its effect on others.

FIGURE 6.2 **Analyzing the problem**

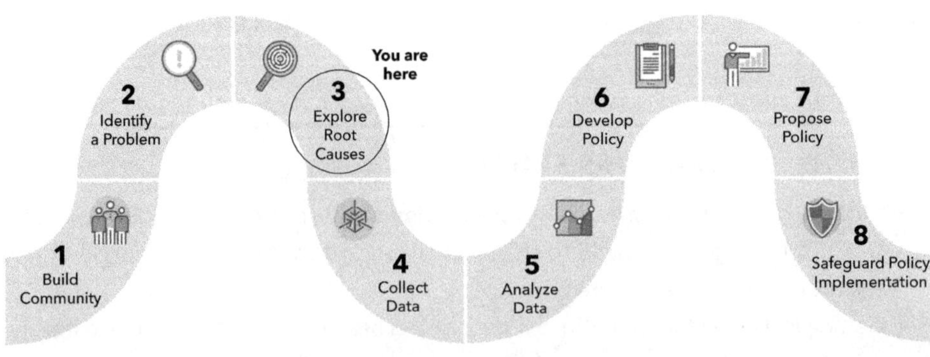

SEVEN

Collecting Data

YOU REMEMBER MARK, the teacher we mentioned in chapter 6. It took a few days longer than Mark expected, but eventually his ESL class came to an agreement about the problem they wanted to dig into: intolerance and hate at their school. The students were angry about the verbal harassment and physical threats that occurred every year on Cinco de Mayo. They shared stories about how a faction of white students brought American flags to school and yelled epithets at Mexican American and Chicane students to "go home" and "go back to your country." They were dissatisfied with the principal, whose response the prior year was to ask police to add patrols to the school on May 5, which they saw as not addressing the root cause. Mark was not sure if he and the students could make progress on this complex problem—and he realized the topic would likely be unwelcome among many of his fellow teachers—but he was happy that his students were fired up.

So the good news was that Mark's class had a topic, but how would they turn that into doing research to inform action? This is a common place to be in the Critical Civic Inquiry cycle. This chapter includes all sorts of ideas on how to get students collecting their own data.

STUDENTS AS KNOWLEDGE PRODUCERS

When the term *research* is used in the classroom, it usually refers to students combing through books or websites. Usually the research topic is bounded by the content aims of the class, such as history or literature, and relies on already published sources. In contrast, research in CCI prioritizes knowledge and lived experiences that typically can't be found online or in the library. CCI projects carry out original social science research to illuminate new and often hidden dimensions of the topic.

At this fourth phase in the project, collecting data (see the graphic road map at the end of each chapter), students engage in some sort of inquiry and data collection to understand more about their question. This is a part of the CCI cycle that aligns effectively with common academic standards, such as reasoning about evidence, critical analysis of sources, the scientific method, and written communication. Depending on the research question, data collection can draw on multiple strategies, such as designing a survey to gather the student body's opinion regarding a school policy, conducting one-on-one interviews with teachers, facilitating focus groups with several students, or observing a particular component of their school environment. Students may also opt to utilize artistic approaches to data collection, which can include but are not limited to photo documentation, video, or depicting issues within the school or community through drawing or painting.

Collecting good data is vital to compelling CCI projects and transformative student learning. For example, a high school sophomore, Gloria, wrote this poem after analyzing survey data and interview responses from her peers' experience taking standardized tests.

> I am so tired of being confused.
> All those years of knowledge,
> and still I lose.
>
> Is it C or B? Should I choose
> A or D?
> I second guess myself; which
> letter will it be?
> This pressure I feel will trample
> me like gravity.

I look at the time, and my
thoughts begin to die . . .
At the fact that I'm still on question 5.

I am tired and hungry, my mind
sees breakfast instead,
I'm so uncertain,
I don't want to take this test.

She and her classmates conducted their own surveys and interviews. Without that data, the rich poem would have never come into existence. This poem, however, is more than just a way to share research findings. It placed the student in a dynamic position where she could thread her understanding of the data with her own lived experience and poetic ability, potentially showing mastery of several standards in one product. The poem itself is a data source, a counternarrative to the way adults typically frame the act of standardized testing. Similarly, a high school senior at the same school created the piece of art shown in figure 7.1, which communicated her experience of her school district valuing test results over student well-being. It similarly weaves deep understanding with art and written communication. Both the poem and the visual art were produced by collecting qualitative data and offering artistic commentary on the findings. Often, however, the youth we work with present survey findings with charts and graphs. While we will touch on surveys later in this chapter, we are excited to see some of the more artistic and personalized methods that students are exploring.

Regardless of the research method, the aim of this phase of the cycle is clear: your students should experience the power and insight that comes with gathering original data and making sense of it in relation to their own lived experience. Too often young people's perspectives are not given sufficient attention in research; that's unfortunate because their insights can provide a new, fun, and needed dimension for understanding.

WHERE TO BEGIN

The starting point for data collection is student experience. Not just any students' experiences, but the experience of *your students* in *this classroom*. The whole raison d'être, the key to unlocking the power and value of student-generated research, is to leverage and critically analyze the lived experience of students.

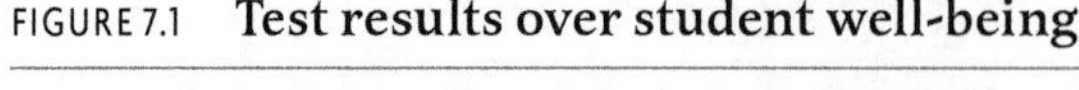

FIGURE 7.1 **Test results over student well-being**

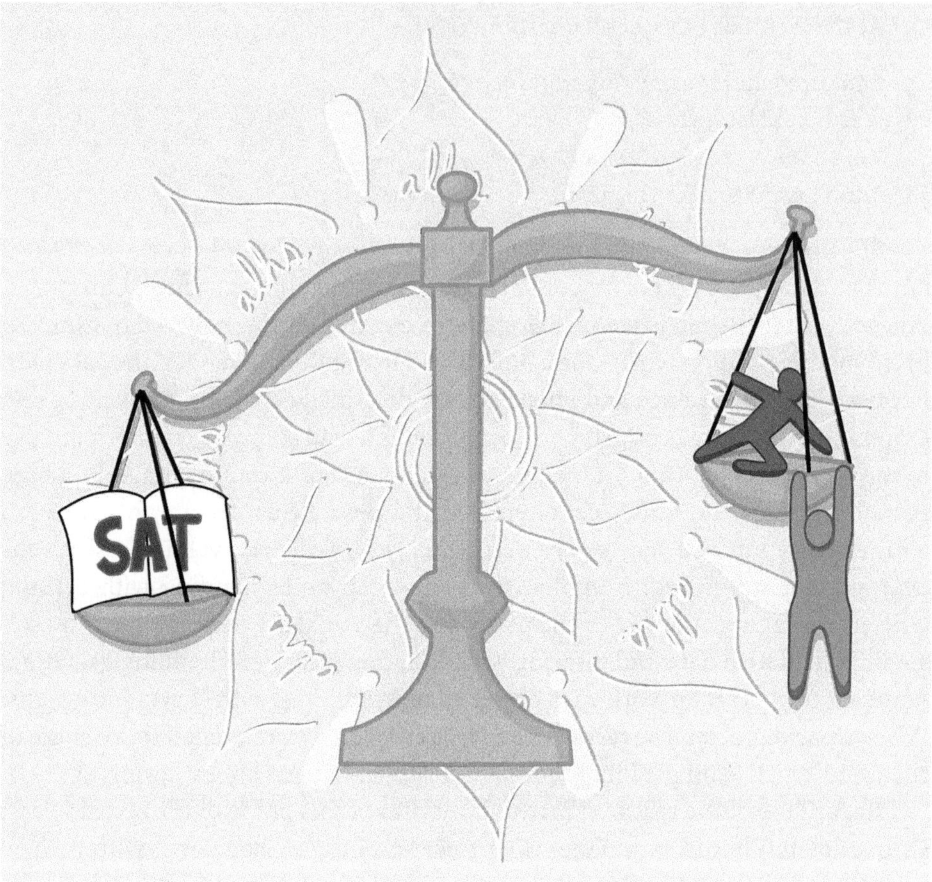

These experiences have value as emergent data, informing preliminary research ideas and guiding where to go looking for more information. We tend to think of this process as a spiral, which starts with the individual, moves to the classroom group, and then extends outward into the population most relevant to your questions.

To return to the example of Mark's ESL class, the topic of intolerance and xenophobia was something students had experienced and talked about as an issue. Students already knew *a lot* about it. Mark invited the students to share their knowledge by writing short essays giving their experiences of what happened on Cinco de Mayo the previous year. As the teacher did in this case, we recommend that a good first step with any data collection process is for students to engage in *autoethnographic inquiry*—aka self-reflection—about their experience of the topic. Think of this as the first coil of the spiral: your own personal lived experience.

The essays were fire. They were gripping and descriptive. They drew on vivid language and used dialogue to bring the reader back to that day. After writing the essays, Mark's students paired up, read each other's, and looked for themes. Eventually, they coded all the essays to identify recurring themes from the day. They turned what had been personal, private memories into the shared discourse of the classroom community. (We'll say more about coding—and other forms of data analysis—in the next chapter.) Their discussion of themes fueled new conversations about why this xenophobia continued to exist and hypotheses about the reasons for the eruption of conflict on Cinco de Mayo. Consider this phase two of the data collection spiral: moving from individual experience to shared themes held among the research team, in this case the collective of researchers in your classroom community.

But Mark's students didn't want to stop at their own experiences. They wanted to find out what the rest of the school thought. Are all the white students racist, or just some of them? How many? Do other students even know what the holiday is about? Collectively they decided to spiral out one more level, to the whole student body of the high school, this time through surveys.

TEACHING TIPS

- Consider setting up a gallery walk of research methods with some examples of student-based products.
- Have youth consider the pros and cons of each method and how it aligns with the story they want to tell.
- When it comes to interviews or surveys, bad drafts are often better than blank pages. Consider creating an example for your students to start with, with explicit instructions that it needs to be revised. Have them work in groups and justify their reasons for changes. Or, download publicly available surveys and have students build from those.

- Don't be afraid to mix methods.
- Common times (like lunch) and spaces (like hallways) can be good for quick bursts of data collection.
- Consider developing clear research plans with students (who is doing what, and by when) and assigning roles (like survey leader or interview coordinator).

(For more, visit TransformativeStudentVoice.net.)

TYPES OF RESEARCH METHODS

While actual methods that students can use to gather data beyond the classroom are endless, when we work with young researchers, we tend to focus on a subset of more familiar methods, ranging from more quantitative and survey based to more qualitative and artistic.

Choosing methods is akin to selecting the right tools for the job. There are a few ways to think about this. In some cases, students will already have a story they want to tell or message they want to convey. In the example mentioned earlier, Gloria and her classmates hoped to express opposition to standardized testing while playing up student humanity. A good question to ask in this case is: what story am I trying to tell (see chapter 10)? That will likely dictate the method you choose. If students don't know yet what their message will be, but instead want to do more research to deepen their understanding and illuminate different perspectives, the question then shifts to: What information do I still need to explore? or Whose voice is not present? While Youth Participatory Action Research elevates the voices of youth, which are typically marginalized, we have seen that within schools, some students' voices rise above others—usually those who excel academically and socially, or those who support the party line of the administration. Many of these methods, then, can be seen as surfacing points of view that are less visible or that counter dominant narratives.

With that in mind, we will now discuss some of our favorite research methods and when to use them.

Archival Research

Definition: Gathering or analyzing information that is already collected and stored somewhere. *Archives* are any existing data set containing information relevant to your work.

Examples: Students in Los Angeles suspected that high schools in wealthy parts of the city offered more college prep classes than schools in low-income parts of the city. They looked at existing data from the California Educational Opportunity Report and were able to create a map showing that their hypothesis was correct: 20 percent more courses offered in the wealthy schools satisfied college prep requirements.[1] If students in Colorado wanted to learn about the history of activism by students at their school, they could go to the Chicano and Latino History Project website to find original sources.[2] If you wanted to compare average teacher salaries across districts around the state, you could go to the Colorado Department of Education to get the information.[3]

When would you use it? If your question is asking about disparities or inequities in systems, or is examining school indicators such as test scores, grades, discipline, or demographics. Honestly, it's always a good idea to start *any* research by looking for what already exists.

When wouldn't you use it? If your question cannot be captured by available data, or if the available data is old or out-of-date.

Surveys

Definition: Using a series of questions to obtain information about the attitudes, beliefs, and experiences of participants. Surveys can be open-ended or can use a rating scale to quantify (put a number value on) attitudes, beliefs, or experiences.

Examples: The US Census uses survey methods to capture information about the US population. A group we partner with in Colorado uses a bilingual student voice survey to capture information from students about their experiences in school.

When would you use it? If you need to capture demographic information (age, gender, GPA) about a group of people or represent the attitudes, beliefs, and experiences of a large group of people. If you want to identify whether a relationship exists between two variables (years in the student voice club and level of activism, for example) or assess change over a period of time (such as improved cultural competence from teacher professional development). If you wish to express the experiences of a large group of people numerically (such as frequency of experience or average grade), or if you think your target audience might respond best to shorter bites of "unbiased" data. (We quote *unbiased* here because we believe youth researchers should have a clear story or agenda for their research. We'll explore this more later.)

When wouldn't you use it? If you're looking to tell a deep, detailed story. Also, we've noticed that surveys are often the only method students use, and this type of data can get stale, lack emotion, and provide limited nuance.

Interviews

Definition: Asking a set series of questions to a variety of people to better understand their personal experiences, beliefs, or attitudes.

Examples: Journalists rely heavily on interviewing experts and other subjects. A job interview could be considered research, as candidates answer the same set of questions. When a number of people are interviewed at the same time, it's called a *focus group*. Whatever the exact approach, interviews should generate deep, personal, detailed responses. It takes time and effort to ask follow-up questions in the interview, and it might make sense to interview the same person multiple times, as each subsequent conversation tends to be more revealing.

When would you use it? If you want personal and qualitative responses. In the testing example mentioned earlier, the youth researchers looked at survey data and then asked a smaller selection of students more targeted interview questions. Those answers helped Gloria write her poem.

When wouldn't you use it? If you want a lot of responses and data quickly; interviewing takes time, and analyzing the data takes even longer. Also, if there might be a risk for the participants if it is discovered who they are—undocumented students, for example.

Testimony/Testimonio

Definition: An act of bearing witness and sharing through first-person oral or written stories.

Examples: College students telling stories from their lived experience to challenge ideas around what knowledge is and who can create it. Latine youth sharing their memories and feelings about discrimination at their high school. Gloria's poem is a sort of testimony about the human side of standardized testing. Think of it as a culturally grounded, first-person monologue; one that can serve as a counternarrative.

When would you use it? If you wish to elicit powerful counternarratives or strongly share the other side of a story that has been silenced.

When wouldn't you use it? When you, as the researcher, want control. Testimonios are all about empowering the subject to share in a way that they maybe haven't been able to before.

Observation

Definition: Observing and recording patterns in your social or natural surroundings, typically through writing notes or tallying frequencies.

Examples: Van Lac, an accomplished YPAR scholar, facilitated a project in which her students wanted to document student-centered and humanizing approaches to discipline in the classroom.[4] The students agreed on three teachers who they felt exemplified their preferred approach, and, with the teachers' permission, they recorded notes of examples that they felt illustrated the teacher approaches. We note that this is not a multiyear ethnography where thousands of pages of field notes are recorded. Instead, these can be completed over a brief time period and can make use of tallies to facilitate data collection (for example, how many times did the teacher praise student effort during the class?).

When would you use it? Observation can be good to document or capture practices that you want to celebrate or dismantle. You could observe how many students walk into the library during lunch time or how many windows are broken in the stairwell. You can document inequities in facilities (by counting broken windows) or educational resources (by comparing how many books are in school libraries). You can also observe behavior, as in Van Lac's example above. Think of this as an attempt to nonintrusively document how things happen in a given space over a given period of time.

When wouldn't you use it? You should not observe humans who have not given permission to be observed. Nor would you want to use observation if it might put your students at risk. Open-ended observations can also generate a lot of descriptive notes that are hard to analyze.

Arts-Based Methods

Definition: Using art and other forms of creative expression to obtain information from participants or community members. Art and creative pieces can be prompted through the use of questions, statements, images, or historical artifacts.

Examples: Your students and their families are experiencing gentrification—storefronts and neighborhood demographics are changing. Arts-based prompts, such as "draw a picture that shows your neighborhood then and now," or "write a poem conveying the new language you hear on the street," could invite people to communicate their complex emotions or evoke feelings. Similarly, if you are studying students' sense of belonging in the building, you could ask them to draw where they feel most valued or their greatest sense of belonging and have them explain their drawing.

When would you use it? This is a great method to use if you want to capture feelings, perceptions, or the complex emotions associated with a topic. This is especially true for people who might have trouble communicating their feelings with words alone, or who might want different ways to express what they are seeing or experiencing. Generally we recommend using one medium per study, just to make it easier to analyze the results. Remember to ask people for their written commentary as well, if possible.

When wouldn't you use it? You might not use this if you want to gather the perspectives of lots of people, because it could be hard to analyze all of the images. Also, if you know your audience (such as a school principal) will want frequencies or percentages, then this might not be the method for your team. Additionally, this won't work if you will be sharing your results in a medium where you will not also be able to include images or art.

WHAT TO AVOID AT THIS STAGE

- *Too much data.* When selecting your data collection method, think ahead to how you will analyze it. It is tempting to want *all* the data, but it's important to focus on what will help you advance your research. If you are interviewing people, how will you record the answers? If you generate hours and hours of audio recordings, those take too much time to transcribe. If you are administering surveys with open-ended responses, how will you analyze the responses? Limit open-ended responses to maybe one or two survey items.
- *Reinventing the wheel.* Good surveys that will give you actionable information are hard to create. Before creating a new one, conduct an internet search for the topic that you care about and build from there.
- *Adultism.* Fight the mindset that youth aren't capable researchers and the inclination to do the data collection for students in the name of moving the project forward. Struggling through hurdles or tensions is part of the research process.
- *Jumping to conclusions.* Even if students know what they want to say before conducting research, let the process play out. New, exciting, and unexpected understandings often surface.

CONCLUSION

Key Takeaways

- Youth are able researchers who collect important data and create important understandings from it.
- In Transformative Student Voice, research is about illuminating youth knowledge and lived experience that can't be found online or in the library.
- When choosing research methods consider the following questions:
  - What story am I trying to tell?
  - What am I trying to find out?
  - Whose voice or experience has been marginalized?

Summary of Research Methods

- *Archival research.* Using existing data to more deeply understand something.
- *Surveys.* Quick and quantitative responses.

- *Interviews.* A series of set questions to illuminate lived experience.
- *Testimonio.* First-person sharings that bear witness.
- *Observations.* Watching and noting.
- *Arts-based.* Using creative ways to collect and share data.

Up Next: Qualitative Analysis

You've collected a ton of data; now what? In the next chapters we offer insights on how to get started with qualitative and quantitative data analysis, aimed at helping youth share the story they want to tell through their research.

FIGURE 7.2 **Gathering information**

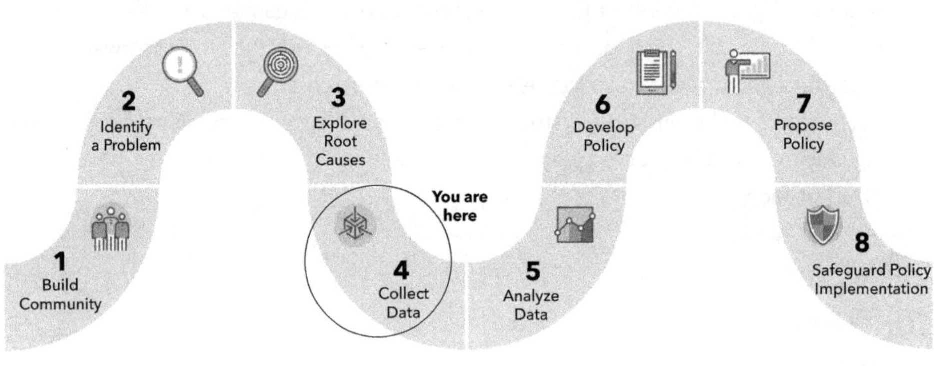

EIGHT

Qualitative Data Analysis

PUT YOURSELF IN THE SHOES OF MARK, from the previous chapters. Your students have gathered a few types of data, one being the personal narratives that they have written about walking through the school building and encountering insults and threats on Cinco de Mayo. These personal narratives, each about one paragraph long, count as *qualitative* data. In addition to the reflection paragraphs, your students have also gathered open-ended responses via a survey. One question, for example, asked, "Besides more police, what can we do to prevent fights or problems on Cinco de Mayo? Explain!" These open-ended responses, although part of a survey, also count as qualitative data, because they come in sentences and words (not numbers).

After celebrating the fact that you've got twelve narratives and eighty-five surveys, the reality sets in: What are we going to do with these? How in the world are we going to make sense of them in a way that is systematic and generates actionable findings? These are good questions. This chapter will share some tips and examples that equip you to move forward. We won't be able to provide a thorough how-to for each of these elements—making sense of interviews, for example, is a different process from analyzing surveys—but we hope to provide enough guidance, examples, and links to resources to give you a running start as the teacher or facilitator.

Data analysis is one of the most challenging parts of Youth Participatory Action Research (YPAR), because it involves three distinct sets of skills, none of which are part of the typical K–12 curriculum or teacher education programs:

- As a researcher, once you have data, how do you analyze it in a credible and trustworthy way?
- As part of a collaborative research team, how do you (collectively) analyze data in a credible and trustworthy way?
- What are the best ways for the teacher to scaffold data analysis for novice researchers (that is, students)?

Typical data analysis manuals focus on the first question. Some advanced articles for specialists get at the second. There are almost no resources that get at the third, but see the endnote for some resources that we found while writing this chapter.[1] We will start with some basic building blocks of skill set number one: analyzing data. We then move into doing this collaboratively, and then how to scaffold this for your students. Onward!

DOING QUALITATIVE ANALYSIS

Qualitative data should help you and your research team tell a story; it should give you deep and rich insights into the experiences and perspectives of your participants. In some cases, frequency or word counts might be helpful (such as how often participants described incidences of bias), but the true power of qualitative methods comes from bringing the experiences of your participants to light.

What Counts as Qualitative Data?

Short answer: anything *not* having to do with quantification, which is to say, numbers. Longer answer: interviews, focus groups, images, artwork, memories, testimonials, statements, social media posts, open-ended answers, report cards, behavior reports, individualized education program (IEP) plans, field or observation notes. We could keep going. The point is that qualitative data can be unusual, unique, creative, and exciting. While that's cool, it can also be really hard for researchers to make sense of the data after they collect it. That's where we, hopefully, can help.

Preparing Your Data

Typically, qualitative data is captured as field notes, open-ended survey prompts, audio recordings, photos, videos, or art. But, as we've mentioned, it can take many other forms. Many qualitative methods require some preparation before they can be coded or analyzed. For example, you might want to upload photos or field notes into a shared space (such as a cloud-based drive) or print copies so the research team can independently annotate documents and share their thoughts.

With audio and video recordings there might be the added step of transcription. It tends to be easier to code a transcription than an audio or video file. Fortunately, there are online tools that can help with transcription or, worst-case scenario, speech-to-text can facilitate the transcription process.

Coding Your Data

Coding describes the process of summarizing large chunks of data into smaller, more manageable pieces. A qualitative researcher might engage in coding to derive larger themes from their data. These themes will be easier to organize and arrange than the raw data of larger quotes or pictures.

To help the reader understand the process of coding, we share the following researcher reflection from Carlos. He recorded this reflection at the end of a meeting where he observed a youth group practicing their speeches for a city council open comment period. The following is a verbatim transcript of the reflection. Throughout this section we will return to this reflection to highlight coding strategies and tips.

CARLOS'S REFLECTION

It was interesting to me that the youth were forced to wait until all the adults had an opportunity to practice. Frida clearly asked if the youth could go earlier, but the young people were forced to wait so adults could practice. Making this worse for me was that many of the adults in the room left after they were done practicing. With Noni talking about youth being the priority of the district, it was sad to see that here students were not even a priority in their own school.

Ian being called out for not having words prepared was also evidence of the hierarchy between youth and adults. At least two or three adults did not have fully formed speeches, but they were not called out.

Inductive coding

An inductive approach, illustrated in figure 8.1, means that you develop new codes based on what you see in the data. When you take an inductive approach to coding, the goal is to let the words of your participants guide the process, rather than starting with predetermined codes. Inductive coding is a nice way to show respect to your participants, since it is their thoughts and feelings that shape the themes that are brought forth from the data.

There are a couple of limitations when it comes to inductive coding. The first is that themes might emerge differently than you anticipated. Therefore, an inductive approach to coding can be more useful in exploratory research—research where you do not have a specific outcome in mind. It might also take longer to make sense of your findings when using an inductive approach, as you try to consolidate and reconcile the opinions or experiences of different participants.

FIGURE 8.1 **Inductive coding**

FIGURE 8.2 **Deductive coding**

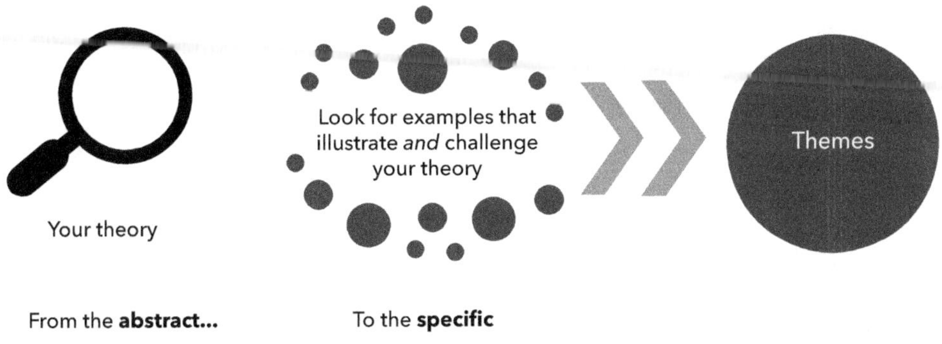

Deductive coding

In this approach, illustrated in figure 8.2, the researcher will use a predetermined set of themes when coding data. This is particularly helpful when you are looking for specific information or experiences. If your research is being guided by a particular theoretical frame or theory, deductive coding is a good approach.

In deductive coding it is a good idea to have a codebook. A good codebook will have your predetermined codes, what the code means or is intended to capture, and an example of coded data that would fall under that code. Having a codebook is a good way to ensure consistency between coders (see table 8.1 for an example).

A drawback of deductive coding is the possibility of missing findings not explicitly covered by your coding structure. Often findings that emerge from the data are more powerful or insightful than those you originally sought to find. To keep this from happening, maybe leave space in your coding structure for emergent themes.

PRACTICE

Using Carlos's reflection, try out inductive and deductive coding strategies.

- Go through inductively (with no predetermined codes) and see what themes you can identify.

TABLE 8.1 **Sample codebook: Coding youth empowerment**

LEVEL 1 CODES (MORE GENERAL)	DESCRIPTION / DEFINITION	LEVEL 2 CODES (MORE SPECIFIC)	DESCRIPTION / DEFINITION
1. Youth-adult interactions	How youth and adults interact, and how that shows up in your data.	1.1 Adultism	Adults engage in differential treatment of youth based on their age, or adults act with greater authority, power, or privilege with respect to youth.
		1.2 Empowerment	Adults treat youth more like colleagues or collaborators; this is more reflective of a partnership approach.
2. Youth voice	How youth express themselves about issues that they care about in different situations or contexts.	2.1 Youth self-advocacy in meetings	Students advocate for a change in agenda or their right to speak during a meeting.
		2.2 Youth advocacy for new education policies	Students speak to policymakers or decision-makers about changes they want to see in their school or district.
		2.3 Youth self-expression through the arts	Students express values, aspirations, or beliefs through creative arts, such as murals, poetry, spoken word, or music.

- Now go through deductively and use the codes *adultism* and *youth advocacy*. See how many coded segments you might identify.
- Reflect on the process: Was one method easier? Did one method produce "better" results, that is, more insightful segments of data?

Coding segments

A good code provides context for the segment of data it represents, so the segment of data should not be too short. If you only code a couple of words, for example, you might miss the context of how or why a statement was made. Let's return to Carlos' reflection for an example. Coding the section of text that reads "evidence of hierarchy between youth and adults" would miss the context of this statement. Whereas if we code the full statement, "Ian being called out for not having words prepared was also evidence of the hierarchy between youth and adults. At least two or three adults did not have fully formed speeches, but they were not called out," we have more context for the idea of hierarchy between youth and adults. The specific example of Ian being critiqued for not having words prepared in advance, while adults were not, gives more specificity and vibrancy than simply acknowledging "evidence of hierarchy."

A good rule is to keep the coded segments somewhere between a couple of sentences and a paragraph long. If the code is too long, it becomes harder to make sense of what is being said by the participant. It might also tempt you to use multiple codes for the same segment of data. The challenge with having segments of data with multiple codes can arise later when you attempt to describe a theme and how it is unique from other themes. If the themes are composed of overlapping data, what makes them truly unique? And worse yet, how do you pick representative quotes that are unique to a said theme?

When coding, it is also important to use codes that clearly describe the chunk of data to which they are assigned. Carlos likes to, when possible, use the words of the participants as his codes. This is particularly helpful with inductive coding or emergent codes—both examples of codes arising from the data and not from a predetermined code sheet. In the example of "Ian being called out for not having words prepared . . ." a good code might be *hierarchy between youth and adults*. This code clearly captures what is happening in the segment of data and uses Carlos's words.

The process of coding

No matter what type of qualitative data you have collected, a good first step is to review all your data before you start coding. This will give you a better sense of the scope of your data—literally how much you have. It will also give you a sense of your timeline, letting you know of things that happen later in the story.

Once you have reviewed all your data and have a general sense of what it contains, you can begin the process of coding. In your first pass at coding, we recommend a line-by-line reading, where most segments of data are coded. There are a few different strategies for how to do this. Possibly the easiest method is to use a physical copy, annotating directly onto the page. You might use different color highlighters (with each color signifying a specific code name) to code segments of data. Alas, this book cannot be printed in color. So, returning to

Using Colors to Code

It was interesting to me that the youth were forced to wait until all the adults had an opportunity to practice. Frida clearly asked if the youth could go earlier, but the young people were forced to wait so adults could practice.

Making this worse for me was that many of the adults in the room left after they were done practicing. With Noni talking about youth being the priority of the district, it was sad to see that here students were not even a priority in their own school.

Ian being called out for not having words prepared was also evidence of the hierarchy between youth and adults. At least two or three adults did not have fully formed speeches, but they were not called out.

Carlos's reflection, we might use the light gray to denote examples of adultism and darker gray for examples of youth advocacy. You could use pink and blue (or whatever you like). The box above shows what this might look like.

Another strategy might be to code digitally. You might, for example, use a spreadsheet program (such as Excel or Google Sheets). As you identify segments of data, digitally copy and paste them into your spreadsheet. To help organize your data, in one column you might have the segment of text to be coded, and other columns can have the name of the participant, the code name, and a description of the code. Using Carlos's reflection and the same codes as the paper example, this would look like table 8.2.

After coding all of your data, you might be tempted to stop. However, it is a good idea to take another pass through. It is helpful to see if data that have a shared code actually work well together. In Carlos's reflection, for example, you want to ensure that the segments coded as *adultism* meet the definition of the code.

If you have engaged in inductive coding, or if you have emergent codes, it is likely necessary to cluster together codes that are similar. This will help you reduce the total number of codes that you have, and it will help you make broader sense of your participants' experience. For example, codes of *grades*, *GPA*, and *As* might be grouped together as *academic performance*. Ben recommends using sticky notes to help with this process. You can write codes on individual sticky notes and then cluster them in small groups, each with their own name. After

TABLE 8.2 **Coding using a spreadsheet**

SEGMENT OF TEXT	PARTICIPANT	CODE NAME	CODE DESCRIPTION
It was interesting to me that the youth were forced to wait until all the adults had an opportunity to practice. Frida, a student, clearly asked if the youth could go earlier, but the young people were forced to wait so adults could practice.	Carlos	youth advocacy	Examples where students advocate for themselves
Making this worse for me was that many of the adults in the room left after they were done practicing. With Noni talking about youth being the priority of the district, it was sad to see that here students were not even a priority in their own school.	Carlos	adultism	Examples where adults either privilege their own voices or dismiss youth perspectives
Ian being called out for not having words prepared was also evidence of the hierarchy between youth and adults. At least two or three adults did not have fully formed speeches, but they were not called out.	Carlos	adultism	Examples where adults either privilege their own voices or dismiss youth perspectives

clustering, you can use a white board or poster paper to draw connections among the clusters and write out the relationships between codes. As suggested by table 8.1, it often makes sense to create two levels of codes—one that is more general, sometimes called a *parent code*, and subcodes that are more specific, sometimes called *child codes*.

Occasionally, you might also want to eliminate codes that do not relate to what you are studying. For example, imagine that you have a code about ice cream and the flavors that participants like, but your study is about discipline practices. Ice cream flavors will likely not help you describe school discipline practices. The recommended total number of codes really varies by how complex your research questions and data set are. But in general, for collaborative coding, you want to keep it simple so you can have some confidence that people are applying codes the same way, which means roughly two to three parent codes and eight to ten child codes. As an upper limit, we recommend no more than five to seven parent codes and no more than twenty to twenty-five total child codes. This is partly because you don't want your coders to have to remember too many variables; your coding will be less reliable if the coders can't remember them all. Also, proliferating codes is often a sign that you are not sure what your focus is or what your core research questions are.

DATA ANALYSIS IN TEAMS

Optimal team size is two or three students looking at a shared data set. More than that and it can be challenging to agree on claims or themes or findings. Let's say you have a class of twenty-five students who are working on a shared question: *What creates a sense of belonging for students in the building?* Let's say you have notes from interviews with twenty students from outside of the class. After completing some initial discussions and meaning-making as a whole group, you identify five themes (codes) to look into more carefully: relationships with teachers, relationships with peers, curriculum and classes, extracurriculars, and physical space. One straightforward approach would be to break the class into teams of two to three to look at each category. It's okay if there are two teams looking at the same category. This means one group would look for examples in the interviews for relationships with teachers, another for quotes describing relationships with peers, and so on.

Managing bias is a controversial issue. On one hand, the reason for being part of YPAR is precisely because students have lived experience (that is, "biases") that ought to inform decision-making. Students bring insight and knowledge by virtue of their position as students. We are not making claims to naive objectivity or neutrality here, as much as you might be pressured to act that way by decision-makers. On the other hand, if you are collecting data from other people, there is an ethical responsibility to represent what they shared with you with some level of accuracy. The data analysis process should not be just cherry-picking the examples one likes and hiding the examples that disagree with your view.

In our experience, young people get this, but it is worth taking time—if you have it—to raise this point with your team. One way is to ask the class, before embarking on the data analysis process, "What stories are you hoping to encounter in this data?" Or, "What change do you hope to make based on what people told you?" Or, "If you were asked these questions, what is your perspective on it?" (Ideally you would have already had this conversation before going out to do interviews.) We recommend making these wishes or desires visible—on poster paper or on a presentation slide displayed for everyone to see. Once those are there, you might ask, "What will you do if you encounter some interviews where people say something different?" And, "How should we handle information that people share that you disagree with?" In our experience, this is a lively conversation that can surface tensions between the youth researchers' goals and the diversity of perspectives they may encounter.

To extend this, you might even share some of the research on human errors in reasoning and scientific inquiry, such as confirmation bias or recency bias. (*Confirmation bias* refers to the idea that we tend to look for information that confirms our preexisting beliefs; *recency bias* refers to the tendency to draw conclusions based on the most recent evidence you saw.) Maybe you set up a challenge to see who can find the most counterexamples in the class, which is to say examples of statements that differ from the majority. Remind people that this is an iterative process, and you may have to return several times to the data to get the story right.

SCAFFOLDING THE PROCESS FOR STUDENTS

Ben loves teaching people how to analyze data. Contrary to popular belief, analyzing data can be the most fun and creative part of the research process.

Evidence Versus Opinion

Data analysis is what distinguishes *evidence* from *opinion*. Sometimes all that a YPAR team has time for is to reflect on their own perspectives, based on their own lived experience, and communicate that. If that's what you do—that's amazing! Sharing the perspectives of a team of young people is powerful in its own right, does not happen often enough, and can sometimes be enough to change the minds of policymakers. But, in some cases, analysis will be key—for example, if you have gathered data from other stakeholders, if your students are hungry to tell a story that represents not just their own experiences but those of their peers, or if you are going to make arguments to an audience that wants more representative or systematic data.

Ben found that students get this distinction intuitively, but if you wanted to scaffold it with a brief role-play, that can be fun too. For example, you might create a scenario where two teams of students are presenting before a decision-making body arguing for funds to be invested in improving their libraries. Team one is given a script that relies only on anecdotes and impressions. Team two is given a script that describes a few types of evidence that they gathered through their research process. The decision-makers (comprised of the rest of the class) are asked to reflect on which team was more convincing. This generates a conversation about evidence and about which types of information are most persuasive.

YOU BE THE JUDGE

Which presentation was more compelling? Why?

Presentation One: When we go to the library, it's hard to find books we need. A lot of people say the library is trash. We found a book in the library that was published in 1973.

Presentation Two: Five students went to the library to check out books for research projects. Of the five students, only two were able to find books relevant to their topic. Also, we pulled a random sample of twenty-five textbooks and found that more than half had been published before 1990. None of us were even alive in 1990!

Pattern Finding

One way Ben likes to start lessons on data analysis is with a simple game of pattern finding, just to prime people on how to play with words and ideas by looking for themes across cases. It starts like this: "I'm going to read a list of words or phrases. If you think you know what the pattern is that unites the words or phrases, stand up. The first person to stand up—and name the accurate pattern—wins." Ben usually starts with simple patterns, like names of cities in Colorado: Denver, Colorado Springs, Boulder. Then he names cities in the United States. Then Ben might purposefully throw a curveball: Denver, Dallas, Detroit. At this point, several people stand up, saying, "Cities that start with D." And then Ben says, "Well, you were impatient and went for the quick interpretation instead of looking across all of your data." He will continue on: Detroit, Kansas City, Miami . . . (the answer is cities with NFL football teams). After establishing this first part, Ben typically moves into slightly more abstract categories, such as by listing movies featuring the same famous actor or actress. He will conclude by saying, "OK, now we're really going to get challenging and will share examples or quotes from the data set we are going to work with." At this point people are ready to roll. Inevitably, the students identify some initial themes at this point and are primed to work.

Modeling a Process

For a sample process, we can consider how teachers are depicted in movies and TV. The purpose of this activity is not only to get people thinking, but specifically to lay out a process that the students will follow with their own data. In essence, through a twenty- to thirty-minute activity, we simulate what the students will do with their data. We start by identifying a data set—in this case movies or TV shows that portray teachers. Once we have a list, we code each text for examples of depictions of teachers. Ben leads the group in an example. Let's take *Freedom Writers*. How is the teacher depicted here? "White savior," "good at teaching," "caring"—these are all responses he has heard. Then they go to the next show or movie, and the next. They start to generate a list of examples. Then, once they have that, the process becomes a bit more open, fluid, and unpredictable. But generally, the idea is to say, "OK, what are some patterns or themes you notice across the examples?" Sometimes people notice how women teachers are presented as either saviors (*Freedom Writers*) or sinful (*Bad Teacher*). Others notice that some depictions imply that teaching is intuitive and does not require formal training (*School of Rock*) or that depictions imply that schools are soul sucking places (*Ferris Bueller's Day Off*).

This conversation, ideally, accomplishes two things. First, it demystifies the process and provides a structured approach that people can draw on. Second, it models critical analysis of text—we're not saying *teachers are x or y* but are instead looking at how popular myths about teachers, including damaging ones, get perpetuated. This is useful in terms of modeling a kind of analysis that can fuel critique and counternarratives. The activity concludes with a list of steps that students are instructed to follow when looking at their qualitative data, whether open-ended survey responses, notes from interviews, or photographs.

PROCESS FOR QUALITATIVE DATA

- Identify the data you will use to answer the question.
- Clarify your guiding questions.
- Get to know your data; read through with an open mind.
- For each data source, look for evidence relevant to your question.

- Once you've come up with lots of different kinds of evidence for each data source, look for patterns and frequencies: What themes do you see showing up across one data source? How many times does that theme show up? What about across data sources?
- Look for outliers that that you deem important or not discardable.
- Tell a story about your data.

FORMING CONCLUSIONS

With qualitative approaches you want to ensure you are making claims based on your data. What do your codes say about your students' experience? You want to be able to point to a specific picture or series of quotes to help reinforce your point. Be careful, however. Make sure that your conclusions are related to your research questions. As we explored before, favorite ice cream flavors may be interesting data but not when the research question involves school discipline. Also, take care to analyze who is represented and, more importantly, who has been excluded from the data. In qualitative research, for example, if the code came from one participant, participants of one identity, or even participants from one school, then the code might not be generalizable. If the code came from several students of different backgrounds and contexts, then the code may be stronger; we would expect to see similar results in similar places.

CONCLUSION

Key Takeaways

- *Model and practice.* Data analysis is new for many students, so showing them a way to do it is paramount.
- *Evidence over opinion.* The data or evidence should lead us to findings. Ideally, we should not let our preconceived notions of the topic dictate our findings.
- *Work in teams.* Data analysis is best done in teams of two or three. Having multiple perspectives is good to ensure data isn't being ignored or cherry-picked.
- *Prepare data.* Written words work best for qualitative coding; that may require transcribing interviews, videos, or audio.

- *Coding*. Choose whether you're using inductive (data as the sole guide) or deductive (using predetermined codes) coding. Then be sure to code or annotate the text in chunks ranging from two sentences to a paragraph.
- *Pattern finding*. This involves reading the codes and their data and grouping them together into buckets of findings. Sticky notes or spreadsheets are helpful.

Up Next: Quantitative Analysis

Now that you've thought about how to work with words, pictures, and other qualitative data, let's do the same with numbers and quantitative data.

FIGURE 8.3 **Making sense of qualitative data**

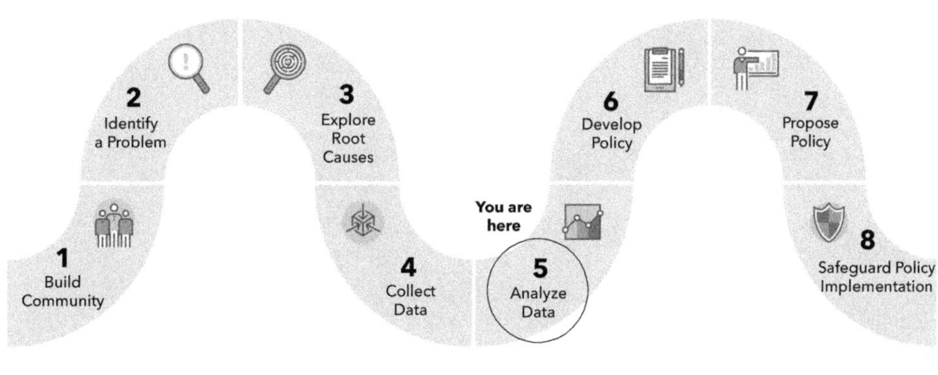

coding. Then [illegible]

[illegible]

[illegible] them together [illegible]

[illegible] helpful.

[illegible] Qualitative [illegible]

[illegible]

[illegible]

NINE

Quantitative Data Analysis

THE STUDENT VOICE TEAM at Creative Arts Academy (CAA), a magnet high school in a suburban Midwest city, wanted to diversify their school. Despite being in an ethnically diverse part of the city, most students at the school identify as white. They hypothesized that various factors contributed to this lack of ethnic diversity at their school, including lack of access to arts curriculum in local schools, the high costs of out-of-school arts programs, and a limited awareness of CAA's existence.

To test their hypotheses, the team designed and distributed a survey for parents whose children were auditioning for admission to the school—all prospective students at CAA are required to audition, and only a select few are invited to attend. The survey asked parents how many arts courses their child had taken in elementary and middle school, how many out-of-school arts programs their child had participated in, how they heard about auditions, and questions about their child's demographics (ethnicity, gender, and socioeconomic status).

The student voice team compiled their data and used means, frequencies, and percentages to present descriptive data on the students who were applying to CAA. A number of findings stood out to the team, including how families learned about CAA and their audition process. Only 16 percent of students had learned about CAA through school communications and outreach efforts. The majority of families learned about the school through friends who attended the school or private tutors who recommended it to students. The student voice team later used these findings to present to their school administration and argue for the need for more targeted outreach efforts in general, but specifically for students of color.

Quantitative methods often appeal to student voice groups; perhaps this is due to familiarity with surveys (most students are asked to complete numerous surveys during the school year), a belief that numbers don't lie, or the sense that administrators have more confidence in statistical results. Given this, knowing how to conduct basic statistical analysis can be helpful. In chapter 8, we described some strategies for how teachers can scaffold and organize the qualitative data analysis process. In this chapter, though, we will focus more squarely on how to do quantitative data analysis. As with the previous chapter, we remain in the fifth phase of our graphic road map.

DOING QUANTITATIVE ANALYSIS

Quantitative data usually comes in or can be represented in numeric form, such as a student's grade point average (GPA) or number of suspensions. Though quantitative findings typically cannot provide the same level of richness as qualitative results, they can be useful for larger data sets and can help you describe means, ranges, frequencies, or percentages. Quick stats review: means and averages are the same thing, frequencies are how many times something happens, and percentages show us part of a whole. Some school administrators and policymakers might give more credence to quantitative analysis either because it is easier to consume or because they believe that it is less biased. Again, we see *bias* as a bit of a loaded term. Certainly, no researcher should ignore or make up data to fit their claim, but we do think that researchers benefit from having a central story, message, or motivation in their work. In that regard, clear direction and bias can be hard to tell apart.

What Counts as Quantitative Data?

Short answer: anything dealing with numbers. Longer answer: survey responses, GPAs, rates (tardy, suspension, expulsion, incarceration), the number of students in AP classes, budgets, distances, heart rates, calories, square footages, noise levels, air pollution in parts per million. We could go on.

Preparing Your Data

Regardless of how you collected your data, you will likely have to do some cleaning up (such as correcting input errors) before actually analyzing. If you collected data using a paper survey, you will want to transfer your data to a spreadsheet (such as Excel or Sheets); using this type of program will simplify your data analysis. It will also be important to decide who will do this data preparation. Is this something that you (the teacher) want to assign to your students, or will it be easier and more efficient to handle it yourself?

If your team collected data online, they might need to download the data. In some cases, the data will download as statements, such as *strongly agree* as opposed to a number *5*. In that case, your team might need to use the find and replace function to change all those strongly agrees to 5s in order to conduct your analyses.

While preparing data, it is also wise to look for bad or missing responses. It might be the case that some respondents did not take the survey seriously or mistyped their response. For example, some responses fall out of a logical range: a high schooler might say they are "69" years old, or might list a nonexistent school for a question like, "What high school do you attend?" If included, these types of errors can lead to bad statistical findings—in the case of the age example, it would make it look like your participants are, on average, older than they really are. With these types of errors, the team should seriously consider deleting all the data from that respondent. If they did not take that response seriously, who is to say they did not goof around on their remaining responses?

Another issue is missing data. Maybe a respondent skipped an item or did not finish the survey. Though some more advanced statistical programs have methods for handling missing data, Excel and Sheets often do not. Once again, the team should consider deleting all data when a respondent does not complete the survey.

A bigger concern would be if participants frequently skip a particular item—this could be a sign that the question is unclear and needs to be revised or that the survey is asking for sensitive information that participants are unwilling to provide. Another potential concern would be a pattern of participants not finishing the survey; in this case, it could be a sign that your survey is too long and needs to be shortened.

TABLE 9.1 **Data cheat sheet**

QUESTION NUMBER	TEXT	LOWEST VALUE	HIGHEST VALUE
1	There is a sense of community in my student voice team	1 = strongly disagree	5 = strongly agree
2	What is your grade level?	1 = ninth grade	4 = twelfth grade

Before beginning your analysis, we recommend creating a cheat sheet. A simple cheat sheet will help keep track of data and what it represents. For example, have columns for the question number, the text of the question, the lowest numerical value and what it represents, and the highest value; we give an example in table 9.1. This cheat sheet will be helpful when you later go back to make sense of the responses.

Basic Statistical Analysis

As the stats nerd—he has a button that proclaims as much—Carlos can attest that in statistics there can be a fascination with conducting complex analyses. Sure, a structural equation model looks impressive in a report, but such analysis require a deep understanding of statistical methods. And they also necessitate more advanced—and sometimes expensive—statistics programs. There can still be great power in conducting basic statistical analyses. Calculating frequencies, percentages, and averages can help a youth voice team in telling their story. To help us visualize some of these methods, we provide a fictional data set, shown in figure 9.1, that captures the ethnicity, GPA, and number of suspensions for ten respondents.

Frequencies

We will begin with frequencies, which describe how often an event occurs or how often your participants gave a certain response. This can be helpful when you are trying to describe your participant pool (how many students identify as Latine, for example) or demonstrate the extent of an issue (how many students of color received suspensions).

Let's say we want to know how many of the students in our fictional data set identified as Latine. Unfortunately, Sheets does not read text (*Latine*) as data. Therefore, as we discussed above, we will first need to recode ethnicities to numerical form. For our purposes, let's decide 1 = Latine, 2 = African American,

FIGURE 9.1 **Basic statistical analysis data set**

	A	B	C	D
1	**Participant**	**Ethnicity**	**GPA**	**Suspensions**
2	1	African American	3.1	0
3	2	Latine	3.9	0
4	3	White	2.7	1
5	4	African American	3.8	2
6	5	African American	2.9	2
7	6	Latine	3.3	3
8	7	African American	3.5	0
9	8	White	3.7	2
10	9	Latine	3.4	1
11	10	African American	3.2	1
12				

and 3 = white. We will use the find and replace function to help us with recoding. See figure 9.2.

With the recoding done, we can now work on our frequency count. To obtain a frequency count on Sheets, you will use the formula =*COUNTIF(range, criterion)*. In our example, range represents the whole of participant responses (B2:B11) and criterion refers to the response we are seeking (in this case 1, since 1 = Latine). This will yield a whole number representing the total number of students who identified as Latine; here, the answer is 3. Check out figure 9.3 for how to carry out this analysis.

Percentages

A percentage describes what proportion of your participants provided a specific response. Percentages can be particularly helpful for describing the demographics of your participants (what percentage of your participants identified as African American) or what proportion of your participants had a specific experience (what percentage of your participants had never been suspended).

For this demonstration, let's stick with that last question. In our fictional data set, what percentage of the respondents had never been suspended? To

FIGURE 9.2 **Find and replace**

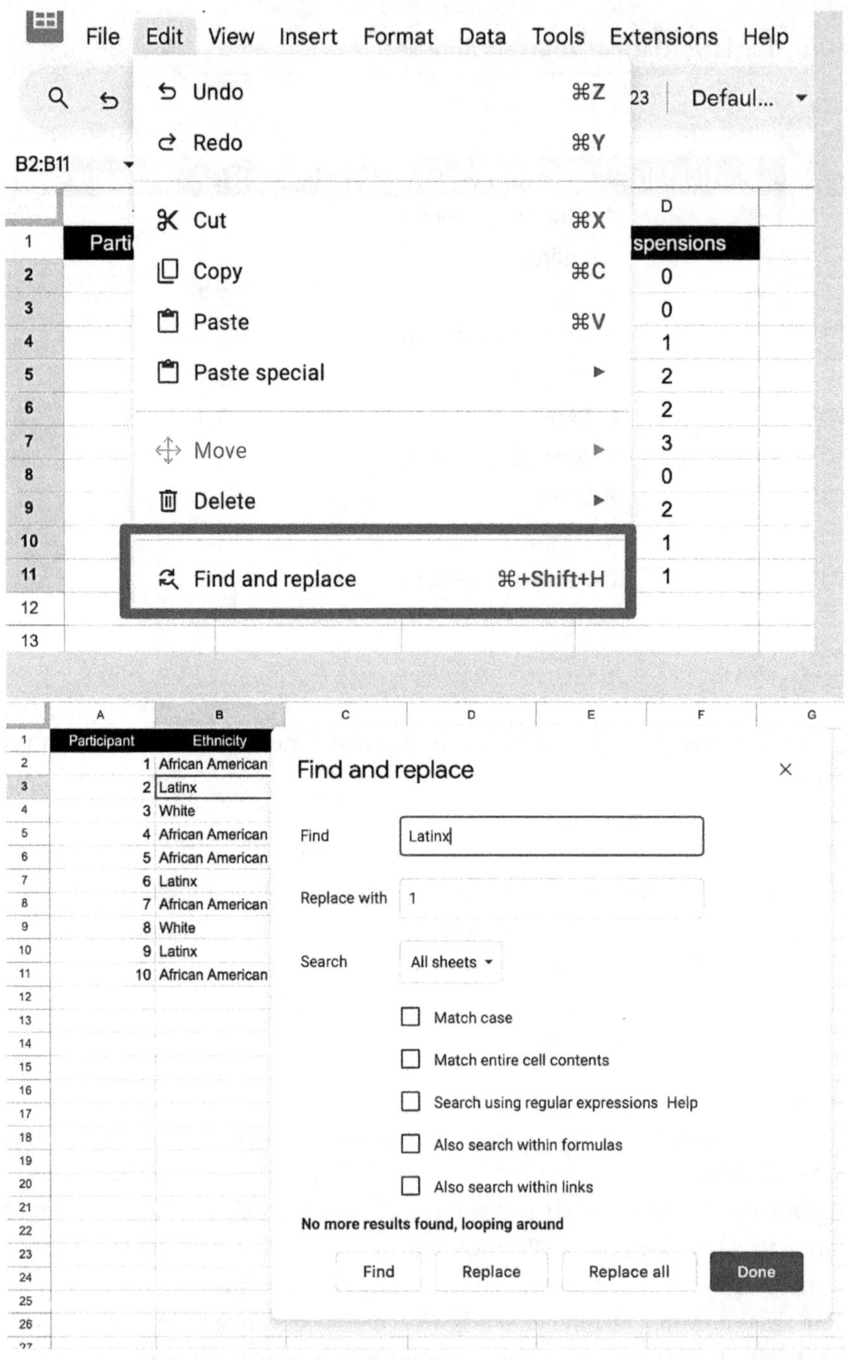

FIGURE 9.3 **Calculating a frequence account**

	A	B	C	D
1	Participant	Ethnicity	GPA	Suspensions
2	1	2	3.1	0
3	2	1	3.9	0
4	3	3	2.7	1
5	4	2	3.8	2
6	5	2	2.9	2
7	6	1	3.3	3
8	7	2	3.5	0
9	8	3	3.7	2
10	9	1	3.4	1
11	10	3 ×	3.2	1
12		=Countif(B2:B11, 1)		

calculate this percentage in Sheets we will use the formula =*PERCENTIF(range, criterion)*. For this question our range is D2:D11 and the criterion is 0. This will yield a percentage; in this case 30 percent of the sample had never had a suspension; figure 9.4 shows this formula in action.

Averages

Without getting too technical, an average gives you the typical response from a larger set of data. Technically it is the number you get by summing all the responses and dividing by the total number of responses. Averages can be useful in summarizing continuous data, such as the age or GPA of participants. It will not be helpful with categorical data, such as ethnicity and gender. Even if represented numerically, the average of gender is meaningless.

Let's keep playing with our data set and seek to get the average GPA of the participants. In this case we will use =*AVERAGE(range)*, where the range is C2:C11. This will yield the average response of participants, in this case a GPA of 3.35. See figure 9.5.

FIGURE 9.4 **Calculating a percentage**

30% ×

D12 fx =percentif(D2:D11,0)

PERCENTIF(range, criterion)

	A			
1	Participant			
2				
3	2	1	3.9	0
4	3	3	2.7	1
5	4	2	3.8	2
6	5	2	2.9	2
7	6	1	3.3	3
8	7	2	3.5	0
9	8	3	3.7	2
10	9	1	3.4	1
11	10	2	3.2	1
12				=percentif(D2:D11,0)

FIGURE 9.5 **Calculating an average**

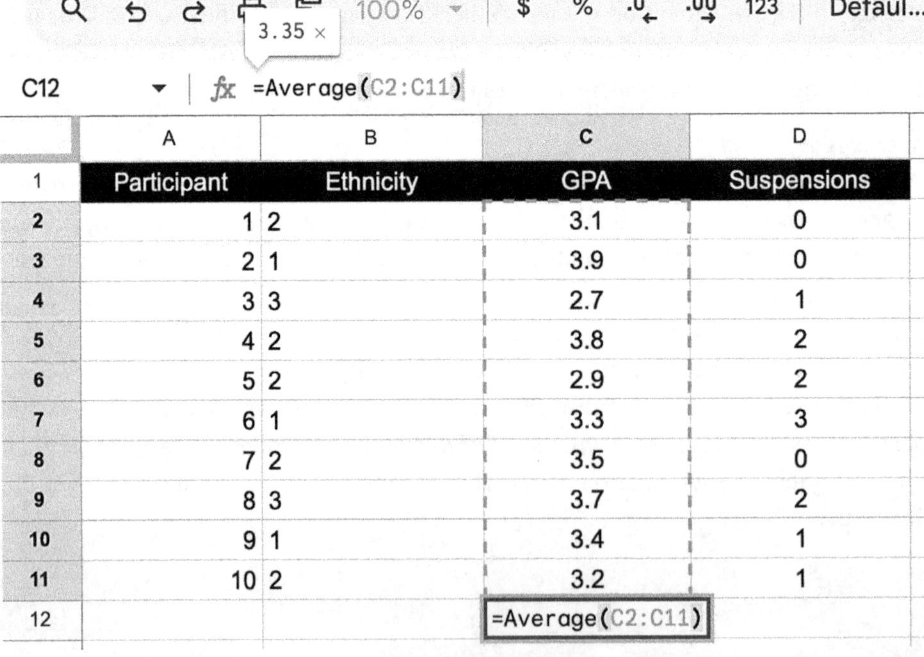

100% $ % .0 .00 123 Defaul...

3.35 ×

C12 fx =Average(C2:C11)

	A	B	C	D
1	Participant	Ethnicity	GPA	Suspensions
2	1	2	3.1	0
3	2	1	3.9	0
4	3	3	2.7	1
5	4	2	3.8	2
6	5	2	2.9	2
7	6	1	3.3	3
8	7	2	3.5	0
9	8	3	3.7	2
10	9	1	3.4	1
11	10	2	3.2	1
12			=Average(C2:C11)	

WHAT TO AVOID AT THIS STAGE

Averages can hide inequities. In a large data set, the use of averages might hide the experiences of numerical minorities. In our fictional data we had an average GPA of 3.35 for the whole group, but when we examine our data by ethnic group (a process called disaggregating), we see that there are only two white students, and their average GPA is 3.2. While this is not a massive departure from the group mean, it does show how an average can hide differences between groups of students.

When you have a larger data set, it will be wise to disaggregate your data—separate it by group—by various demographic indicators such as gender or ethnicity to assure that your larger averages are not hiding differences between student groups.

More Advanced Analysis

There are various other statistical analyses that are possible with proper training and statistical packages. We will briefly touch on the purpose and cautions for correlation and difference tests but will not provide the same level of detail as we did in the analyses described above. If you are interested in these types of analysis, it might be wise to reach out to a statistics instructor or potentially someone in your district's research and evaluation team.

Correlation is a strategy to demonstrate the relationship between constructs; in our fictional data set, we might be interested in the correlation between GPA and suspension. The caution here is to resist making a causality argument—just because constructs are related does not mean one causes the other. A commonly given example is outdoor temperature and ice cream consumption. There might be a relationship here, but it being hot outside does not mean you are definitely buying ice cream—Carlos likes ice cream regardless of the outdoor temperature.

A difference test is used to assess if there is a statistically significant difference in the average answer given between two groups. Back to our fictional example, we might be interested if there is a difference in suspensions between white and Latine students. Difference tests can also be useful in pre- or posttesting (in which we assess a construct prior to an intervention to establish a baseline, then repeat the same assessment after the intervention to evaluate if there is a difference in scores). The challenge here becomes matching up respondents in the pre- and post- contexts. There is also the assumption that no external forces are contributing to differences in scoring. Going back to the example of suspensions between white and Latine students, if administrators and teachers are biased, that could lead to Latine students being suspended more than their white counterparts.

FORMING CONCLUSIONS

In quantitative methods, conclusions should be derived from the results of our statistical analysis. Begin with identifying interesting frequencies, percentages, and averages. In the case at the start of the chapter, the student voice team was shocked that such a small percentage of families had learned of CAA from school-based communications. The conclusion they drew from this was that the school was not doing sufficient outreach and recruitment—a point they could directly support based on their statistical findings. When the student voice team shared this finding with their school principal, it also made an impact on him.

PRINCIPAL REFLECTION

Anderson Donalds, principal, *Creative Arts Academy*

I used a portion of the student voice team's presentation in my discussions with the district. I explained how 84 percent of school applicants heard about CAA from sources other than the school. I used this to justify needed changes in support of student recruitment. Specifically, the need to improve pathways from district schools to our high school, including expanding our middle school program. Having this data aided CAA in securing funds to purchase a new building and, thus, expanding our school's middle school enrollment.

Remember not to overgeneralize your findings; the findings might be different if you surveyed students from other schools or in a different state. Your statistics give you a snapshot for one group of participants at one particular point in time. Some students might feel that acknowledging this point could be seen as a weakness in your results. In many cases, though, recognizing this point can help your team position itself when it faces opposing data or counterarguments. You can also use statistics to compare groups over time. Perhaps survey results at the beginning of the year might be different than at the end. Typically, researchers use this to show some sort of growth over time (a tardy rate improving from one quarter to the next, for example).

We mentioned this before, but we think it bears repeating: in quantitative research, it can be helpful to disaggregate data to ensure that the experiences of marginalized students are not being lost. Make sure to compare statistics across genders, ethnicity, language, and socioeconomic status. In other words, data is best when it is holistic and inclusive.

CONCLUSION

While we have written about qualitative and quantitative data analysis as totally separate things, that isn't always the case. Researchers often run mixed-method studies in which they may use, for example, both surveys and interviews. Often quantitative findings from a survey can point out interesting or confusing points. In that case, it might be worth interviewing the survey respondents to find out more of the story. For example, in examining survey results, you discover that girls who speak Spanish reported feeling like they don't belong in school. To better understand those answers, you could request to interview all the girls who spoke Spanish who took the survey. They could certainly say no, and you would have to honor that, but if they agreed, you could ask deeper questions to understand the root causes of their lack of belonging.

Key Takeaways

- *Prepare data.* Often surveys use words, like *strongly agree*, but most stats programs work solely with numbers. Be sure to assign numerical values to any words in your data. Be on the lookout for patterns of missing data; this could be a sign that your survey is too long or that questions are hard to understand.
- *Cheat sheets.* A simple cheat sheet will help you keep track of your data and what it represents. Consider including columns for question number, the text of the question, the lowest numerical value and what it represents, and the highest value.
- *General cautions.*
  - *Keep it basic.* Frequencies, percentages, and averages are basic statistics, but in most cases they yield interesting insights and findings.

- *Data elevates experiences.* In most cases, students are conducting research to attach youth experience to a problem or issue. That mission should drive data collection whether students are analyzing their own lived experiences or those of their peers.
- *Don't cherry-pick.* Ignoring data you don't agree with or elevating data that doesn't fit with the rest of your research isn't at the heart of what we're doing. Data should be looked at holistically to make claims.

- *Consider inclusion.* The best research empowers a variety of people to share their thoughts, opinions, and experiences. To intentionally or accidentally exclude certain genders, races, languages, and more pollutes the data and the entire TSV project.

Up Next: Telling Your Story

Now that you've arrived at some compelling findings from your data, it's time to think about how to best communicate your research to adults in power.

FIGURE 9.6 **Making sense of quantitative data**

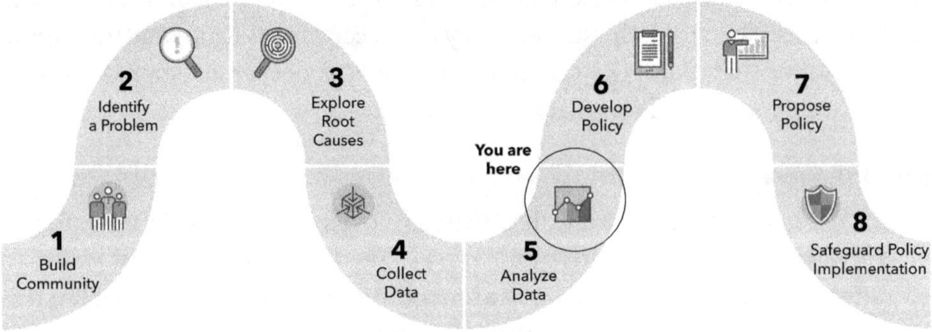

TEN

The Story You Want to Tell

with Bea Salazar

YOU'VE LIKELY FOUND OUT SOME COOL THINGS from your analysis. Now it's time to communicate those findings. This starts with getting crystal clear on the story you want to tell and the voices you hope to center.

REFLECTION ON DATA ANALYSIS

It pays for you and the students to refresh yourselves on what the students have done. They have already isolated a problem, conducted a root cause analysis, and crafted a counternarrative. Then they collected a lot of information and made sense of it through qualitative and quantitative analysis. What exactly were those findings—patterns, themes, claims? Whose voices were centered? Whose may have been excluded? With these questions clearly addressed (this may require more research), you're ready to consider how to share findings in a way that supports your specific mission in this work. Why did you tackle this problem in the first place? What were you hoping to say or change? Being clear on what you set out to accomplish can help dictate the research story you tell.

At New Outlook Academy, which we featured in chapter 2 for their innovative leadership structures, the students had been researching inequities in extracurricular activities offered across the school district. New Outlook is a *pathways* school, meaning it focuses on credit recovery and serves students who have been forced out of other schools. Because of this focus on quickly gaining credit and graduation, pathways schools, including New Outlook, don't offer many extracurricular activities—no dances or pep rallies, for example. Their school is an old office building, and the gym and cafeteria are former office spaces converted to allow for exercise or dining. The young people began to connect the dots between their identity and their lack of opportunities. Most of their classmates had struggled at previous schools. Most of their classmates lived in poverty. Most of their classmates identified as Black or Brown. The students began to find their story: while pathways students may have struggled in the past, they still deserve a well-rounded education on par with what traditional high schools offer.

FINDINGS AS STORY

After data collection and analysis, your findings from the data can become overwhelming to organize. You, as a team, might have quantitative data in forms of surveys, reports, and district numbers. You might have collected data in qualitative form through surveys, interviews, or even historical data. You might have done both. Figuring out the most important parts of your results to communicate can be one of the most daunting pieces of the process. To help with this, we encourage you to view findings as a way to tell a story—the story that you have identified through the root cause analysis.

Now that you have collected the data, take a step back and ask yourselves: what does the data tell us, and how can it help us tell our story? This is going to be a key question as you move through telling the story of your findings. Gaining clarity on what your data tells you is the first step of setting up your story.

At New Outlook, the students collected a lot of different data. They first sought their classmates' opinions and experiences through surveys and interviews. They found that a majority of students felt like they carried a "bad kid" label that made them feel unimportant and unheard. The youth researchers then met with the school administration to share the results from their survey and interviews and to better understand why New Outlook offered so few extracurricular opportunities. The administrators blamed the district's funding formula for pathways schools, which tended to serve smaller student populations and therefore receive less funding. So the students followed up with district personnel to find out more. The youth then surveyed other pathways schools in the district and found their experiences to be similar—the schools offered very few if any activities. At the same time, the student researchers planned a Halloween dance, the first dance in at least ten years, according to their research. More than 90 percent of the student body attended. The youth researchers had learned some important things: students showed interest in wanting more extracurricular activities, but district funding mechanisms appeared to be blocking the way. They needed to find a way to make this clear and compelling for district power players like the superintendent and school board members.

Connecting the Data to Your Story

We hear a lot about how researchers should be unbiased. While it is important for researchers to not falsify or ignore data, we believe that youth benefit from having a clear agenda or stance in their research (what some might consider bias). To that degree, and we're talking to the young people here, what is the story *you* want to tell? What, explicitly, do you want to say, share, and show to your audience? Included in that is exactly what you want your audience to do: email a principal, fill out a survey, show up to a protest. What, implicitly, do you want them to leave feeling? If you can appeal to the audience's ethics *and* emotions, you stand a better chance of aligning them to your cause.

To get started, it first might make sense to sort yourselves into smaller groups. This process can be hard for groups of two to five people and *really hard* for groups of fifteen to twenty. Two or three people is often ideal. In those small groups, identify one or two points that you want people to take away from your story. Those people—the ones you want to reach with your story—become your audience; they matter. We'll go deeper into this in the next chapter, but who is your target audience, what are their values, and how could your research story best appeal to them? An opening that hooks the audience's attention is important, and we'll go deeper into that in chapter 13. But with this specific issue, how are you hooking the audience throughout the story and presentation? We've often seen this happen with testimonials, calls and responses, visuals, and more. As you set up the story, again return to those feelings you want to evoke in the audience. Do you want them to laugh? Do you want them to feel shocked? Do you want them to engage? The data you've chosen and the story it tells should align to those feelings.

In the next sections, we share some considerations around building this story, including choosing the best survey data and open-ended responses, visualizing that data, and thinking through presentation modalities. Beyond that, though, youth should trust themselves in telling stories that are appealing. Think about your own experiences. What elements do you think are important in stories? What keeps you interested and makes you want to take up the call to action?

NEW OUTLOOK'S PRESENTATION

The student researchers at New Outlook presented at a district event. The audience included the superintendent, school board members, students, and other community stakeholders. This is an outline of their argument and approach:

- *The hook.* A student asked the audience to imagine their prom. What did it look, smell, feel like? After allowing time for brainstorming, the student showed an example of New Outlook's prom. The slide featured a spinning error message. New Outlook doesn't have prom. The students in the audience gasped. The next slide featured New Outlook's pep rallies; a meme read, "Sorry kid, try again." New Outlook has no pep rallies.
- *The images*. The students then took the audience on a tour of the school, showing images of the gym (a few weights in a cramped room) and the cafeteria (a small room with a few tables).
- *The story*. The engaging hook and powerfully stark images had quickly captivated the audience's attention. Next, the students laid out their thesis, the story they wanted to tell. At New Outlook, the students said, "We are consistently forced to engage in a second-class education when compared to the traditional schools. This is due to the fact we lack a variety of academic and social opportunities." They then listed out the things the school didn't offer and compared it to other schools.
- *The demand.* To fix the problem, the students proposed a budgetary approach where the sixteen pathways schools in the district would pool money and receive added district support to offer collective dances, sports leagues, and even share art and music teachers. The students also proposed a minimum bar for school activities. They requested that *every* school offer at least four electives per term, four sports offerings per year, four extracurricular clubs, and two school-sponsored events (such as dances or pep rallies).

Choosing the Best Data

You may have quantitative or qualitative feedback or both. Whatever data you have, it's important to choose the best or most aligned data to the story you're telling. We are not asking you to cherry-pick here (that is, do not ignore or disregard data that disagrees with your conclusions, but do select the quotes or data points that speak to the story you want to share). As you begin to analyze your data, you will see patterns arise. In many instances, these patterns highlight and connect to the story you want to tell. Select the data that best supports your story among those patterns.

SHARING DATA AND FINDINGS

Finding ways to both edit and show your qualitative and quantitative findings is important. You certainly don't want to just dump everything on the audience.

Choosing the Right Data

As the previous chapter on quantitative analysis mentioned, start with conclusions from your data. With each conclusion, take the time to connect it to the story you want to tell. The youth from chapter 9 did that with their quantitative data around recruitment, and it more clearly exposed a problem to their principal. Had they shared different data, such as attendance or grade point average, for example, it would not have been so clearly aligned to their story—and likely would have confused the principal.

Similar thinking applies to qualitative data like open-ended responses or interview recordings. Nothing is more powerful in qualitative research than the direct words of your respondents. But, like seasoning in food, quotations should be used judiciously. Choose only the most powerful quotes (or even parts of quotes) to drive home your point. Again, how you present this is key. You don't want the audience to spend several minutes squinting at a lot of small text on a slide. In this way, you will need to play the role of editor, first by deciding *which* quotes to share and then isolating the most important part of the quote that will most solidly land with the audience. Chapter 8 offers extensive advice on qualitative analysis, including using detailed data to land on concrete conclusions, but choosing the right quotes for a presentation requires a slightly different skill.

Before his time as a teacher, Dane was a newspaper reporter who *loved* quotes—maybe a little too much. An editor once told Dane that in a few stories, Dane's voice got lost in all the quotations from his sources. The editor demanded that Dane cut all but three quotes. Having no idea how to pare down his beloved writing, Dane printed out the story and annotated it, numerically ranking the impact of each quote. He read each one in depth and then examined it in the context of his thesis. Only the strongest and most aligned quotations made the cut. Sure, some really good stuff (in Dane's opinion) was cut out of the story, but he couldn't deny that the forced scrutiny and close editing of the quotations made the story clearer and, ultimately, more powerful.

We don't want you to lose your voice, but we advise doing something similar. First figure out roughly how many quotes you will need in your presentation. You will most likely need some for a qualitative analysis or open-ended response slide about your findings, but also consider using strong quotes throughout the presentation as mile markers in your research story—maybe your best quote as a hook, another related to the problem near the middle, and perhaps one as a closing. So, we're talking three to five quotations tops. If you have ten great quotations from your research, consider setting up a *chalk talk* where the quotations are posted on the walls along with the thesis or summary of your research story, and have your colleagues read each quote, comment on them, and rank them in terms of their alignment and support of your story.

Choosing the Best Quotes

Similar to using too many quotes or throwing too much data at the audience, presenters can often run into problems using quotations that are too long. Isolating the most important part of the quote will make the biggest impact on the audience. For example, we at TSV recently wrote an article about levels of student voice. Here is a quote from Zack, a high school senior involved in various leadership classes, that we wanted to use:

> I'm on both student council and the student board of education. Student board is more about creating something to make a big difference in the school as they see as having a big, negative impacts on students. Making the school a better school to go to, I guess. Student council is making the school a little better than it already is. In student council, we try to promote school spirit and build fun. Student board is more about making sure the

> school is safe and fair. It's nice being on both. I can see both perspectives. I'll definitely say, though, that student board feels more like a family. Student council feels more like a class. In both classes, I have fun.

While Zack shares several awesome thoughts in the quotation, his exact words might leave the audience slightly confused. He jumps back and forth between the two classes, and he may not be as focused and clear as our audience needs. No shade to Zack at all! Interviews are conversations, not speeches, so it makes sense that Zack is finding his way in this response. As presenters, though, it's our job to use Zack's words to quickly and powerfully back up the story of our research. In this case, we as authors were hoping to show how programming like student board may have a deeper impact on students and schools than something like student council. Here's what we wrote:

> Zack also took the Student Voice and Leadership class after one of his friends recruited him. He described the class's aim as making "a big difference in the school" by ensuring "the school is safe" and addressing problems that have "big, negative impacts on students." The work around the school rating and leveraging student experience in the poem made for a trusting and vulnerable learning space. As a result, Zack said, the class felt "like family."[1]

As you can see, we definitely used Zack's ideas and exact words, but we edited out some of his language and added our own more direct phrasing. For a presentation, we suggest editing this down even further. If we were to present this, we might place two partial quotes from Zack in tension on a slide: "Feels like a class" versus "Feels like a family." We could then contextualize his words with a brief explanation, connecting the quote to the story of our research.

Choosing How to Visualize the Data

Making the data come to life will be important. There are millions of ways to do this, but a few questions should guide your thinking. Think about the ways you like to see data be presented or even past presentations that you've seen. How was the data presented to make an impact? Did the presenter or author use charts and graphs? Did they use photographs or color? What made their data interesting to their story? Conversely, was there a time where you sat through a data presentation and were uninterested? What would you have liked to see? What did you not enjoy about the presentation?

Data is a tool to help you bring your story to life and *show*, not just tell your audience why they should care. By using visual elements like charts, graphs, and maps, data visualization tools provide an accessible way to see and understand trends, outliers, and patterns in data.[2] It's important because it:

- simplifies the complex information from your research,
- helps you analyze your own data, and
- helps you identify areas for improvement.

The sidebar provides some guiding questions as you consider how to visualize your data.

VISUALIZING DATA

When considering how to present data, information, and quotes, think about the following:

- *Relevance.* Do we know what we want to say? Is it aligned with the rest of our work (problem, root cause, counternarrative, research plan, findings).
- *Precision.* Are we hyperclear in our messaging? Is our story coming across clearly? How much time do we have? Is there too much on each slide?
- *Completeness.* Does the visualization highlight all of the important data or information points? Is anything big missing?
- *Presentation.* Does my presentation both look good and clearly share the information? Do we need to make it look better? Do we need to simplify the design and focus on the message?

The New Outlook students did an awesome job of visualizing their problem and findings by sharing images that highlighted the lack of opportunities at their school. The hook cleverly pulled on the audience's heart strings when the students revealed that they had no prom and many of them hadn't ever attended a dance of any kind. The images that followed, showing the gym and cafeteria, further visualized the problem for the audience, allowing them to connect with the youth. The students chose not to share their survey or interview data. They felt like the images were their best options, and that they spoke more loudly than charts or quotes. With the audience hooked, the youth clearly and succinctly defined the problem and made demands of the district. They did share charts later in the presentation to show that the problem at their school was also an issue at others. But, for the most part, the only data they shared was visual, and they chose to lead with it.

CHOOSING A PRESENTATION MODALITY

Now that you've considered how to visualize your data and share respondent quotes in powerful ways, choosing how to present this information is key. In the program we support in Colorado, students are asked to deliver policy presentations to adult power players. Most choose to use slides or other visualizations. New Outlook used slides. Increasingly, we've seen video utilized both as hooks and as ways to show context or findings. We've seen youth turn to social media as a way to share their research stories and policy demands. We're also hopeful that youth will increasingly follow New Outlook's lead and turn to art and other creative methods—images, music, installations—to share their research journeys.

A key consideration in choosing a modality, however, is *to whom* you will be presenting. The next two chapters examine finding the right adult power players to target and figuring out ways to build alliances with them.

PRESENTATION SUMMARY

- The story we're trying to tell is . . .
- The best data or information points supporting our story are . . .
- Open-ended responses or quotes also support our story by . . .
- We will share our story by using . . .

CONCLUSION

Key Takeaways

- Your research findings should help inform a story you want to tell in your research.
- Choose only the best data to present, and make sure it is aligned to your research story.

- Visualizing data can help for engagement, clarity, and impact.
- Consider how to best present your findings and research story for your context.

Up Next: Power Mapping

Now that you've figured out the story of your research, it's time to present it to somebody who can make the change you want. Chapter 11 shares the idea of *power mapping* to figure out whom to target.

FIGURE 10.1 **Telling your story**

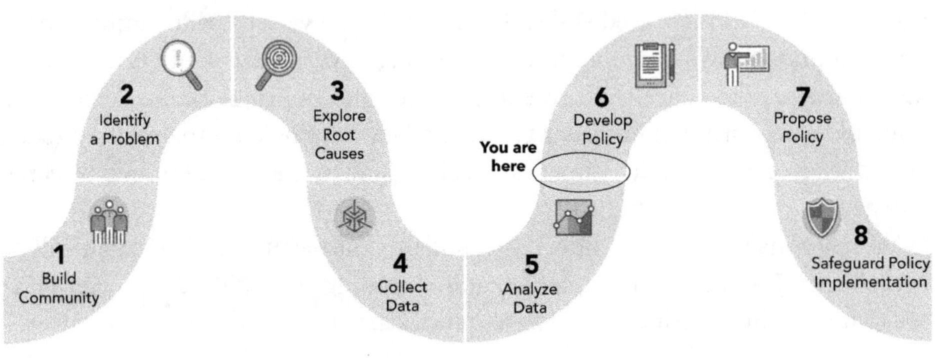

SECTION FOUR

Claiming Power and Voice

YOU'VE GOT YOUR TOPIC AND the findings from your research. You have a sense of what you want to change at your school. Now it's time to develop the skills of democratic participation and voice. This section shares tips from community organizing and civic engagement to equip students to formulate policy arguments, develop alliances, and find the right decision-makers to engage with their ideas. Beware of risks around how student voice can be dismissed or tokenized.

ELEVEN

Mapping Values and Power

IN 2007, WHEN SHELLEY DID HER DISSERTATION RESEARCH on student voice in school reform, she interviewed eighty students across twelve schools—including wealthy, white suburban schools, specialized programs for teen parents or credit recovery, urban schools with students at the intersection of race and class. In all cases, students could identify equity issues in their schools and name possible solutions, but they did not believe that there was anything they could do about it. They just said, "It is the way it is." That ignited in Shelley a fire to figure out how to work with young people so they could see the possibility of change and develop the skills to make change happen. It's pretty easy to get students to identify what's working and what's not. It's a bit more challenging to develop a plan to research the problem, gather data, and make sense of it. Then it gets really hard: what to ask for, how to ask for it, and who to ask. And that is where we start this chapter: figuring out who has power, what they value, and how to tap into that to get them to make the changes you want to make.

WHAT, HOW, AND WHOM TO ASK

Once you've defined your problem, collected your data, and analyzed your results, you are ready to ask for what you need. We've previously shared some details about the Deerfield TSV club, the high school students who surveyed their peers about experiences with microaggressions. They collected more than five hundred responses, analyzed their data, and identified three themes: the prevalence and type of microaggressions experienced, a lack of trust in the adults to respond to the incidents, and the frequency of students being bystanders to these incidents. They then had to make a choice about what to ask for. What would it take to address these three problems? They wanted to have everyone in the school learn more about microaggressions and develop skills to respond, so they started by looking for opportunities to do that. They learned about how teacher training worked in the district (five full days each year, with the assistant superintendent in charge of planning the schedule). They discussed the role of the equity council in helping develop materials for teachers related to equity issues. The students identified their school's "character education" blocks as an opportune time to have discussions with students about these topics, and they determined which teachers were on the committee that developed those lessons. They chose to address the problem of teaching both adults and students in two ways: first, by working with the equity team to develop training for teachers and, second, working with the character ed team to develop lessons for students. In this example, the district was small—about sixteen hundred students—with an equity council that was fully supported by the administration, so they were able to go directly to the people who were responsible for the areas where they focused their intervention, resulting in a less formal process of mapping power and building alliances.

In another example, mapping the people, power, and potential alliances was a bit more complex. In the wake of the Black Lives Matter movement in the summer of 2020, students in schools across the nation began talking about the lack of representation of Black lives in the curriculum of their schools and the reality that what *was* included was often either the negatives (enslavement) or the same small handful of "heroes" (Rosa, Martin, and Harriet). They also pointed out the fact that information about Black history was often relegated to February, Black History Month. A group of current and former students in the Summit School District came together to figure out how to raise this issue. They knew that they wanted to engage the school district but also the township, so they began by identifying key players. They identified the Summit Equity Initiative—a group of local community members who were raising awareness around town about a range of issues—as a possible ally. They identified the key power players—the mayor, city council members, police chief, school board members, and superintendent. The students crafted a letter demanding a community conversation and, with the help of the equity initiative group and Shelley, a professor at a local university, began to draft a plan for what the conversation would look like. In other words, the youth demanded the district hold a meeting but did not cede the planning control to the adults. Instead, the young people led the planning in the intergenerational group.

Mapping the Larger Issue

There are a range of activities you can use to map the power, the people, and the issue. You might start by mapping the issue—start with a concept map, where you identify *who cares* about the issue, *who is impacted* by it, and *who is implicated* in the issue and the solution. Returning to the example in the chapter opening, the concept map (see figure 11.1) shows how the group started

FIGURE 11.1 **Sample concept map**

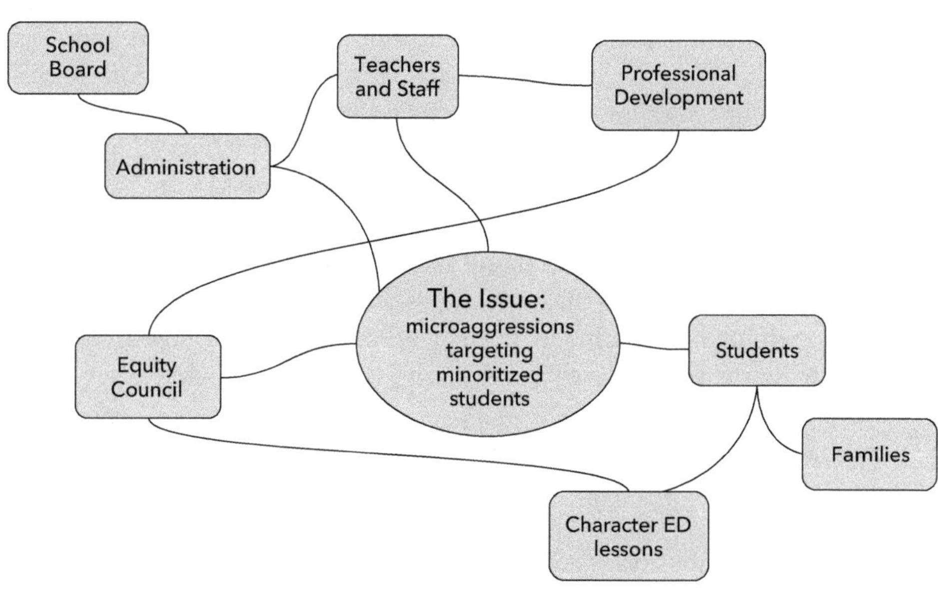

to identify these *whos*. Once they had the graphic created, they started adding details: Who were the people in each group? What did they care about? How were they impacted by the issue? How could they be a part of the solution?

Thinking About Policy

When we say the word *policy*, you might think about big federal policies, like the Every Student Succeeds Act (ESSA) or Individuals with Disabilities Education Act (IDEA), and think that you can't influence those. We want to turn our attention, though, to smaller policies, the kind that are created in classrooms and schools, the kind that might help us get what we need done. This is a time to just generate ideas—name all the policies you can think of that are related to your issue. In the example above, where the issue is about microaggressions, it might have been helpful to look at the policy against harassment, intimidation, and bullying to find out what the responsibility of teachers, administrators, and staff are for reporting and investigating complaints. The group might have looked at the employee handbook to see if there existed employment policies that would be relevant to their request for teacher professional development. They could look at evaluation policies to see if there are items in the evaluation realm that were connected. And they could look at the policy the district had that required all students to participate in monthly character education sessions. Your school district website is a great place to start looking for policies. They should be linked there, often under the board of education page.

Identifying Allies and Opponents

Once you've mapped the issue, you can identify the people connected to it. You can use a graphic, like the one in figure 11.2, and sticky notes. For each of the areas mapped above, identify the key players—write their name on a sticky note, and place them on the grid based on the level of influence or power that they have to impact the issue or your solution and the degree to which they are in support or opposition.

You might also create a custom graphic, like the example in figure 11.3, that includes what *type* of influence the people have, along with their commitment to the work.

Finally, you might do a *six degrees of separation* activity, in which you take all the people you have identified and map the relationships between them. This can help you figure out who can influence someone you need on your

FIGURE 11.2 **Mapping your allies and opponents**

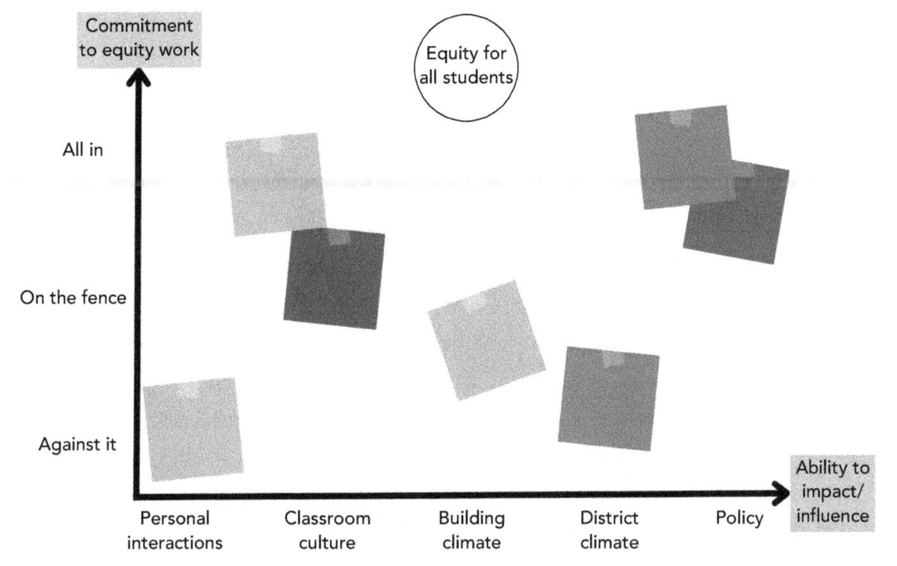

FIGURE 11.3 **Influence grid**

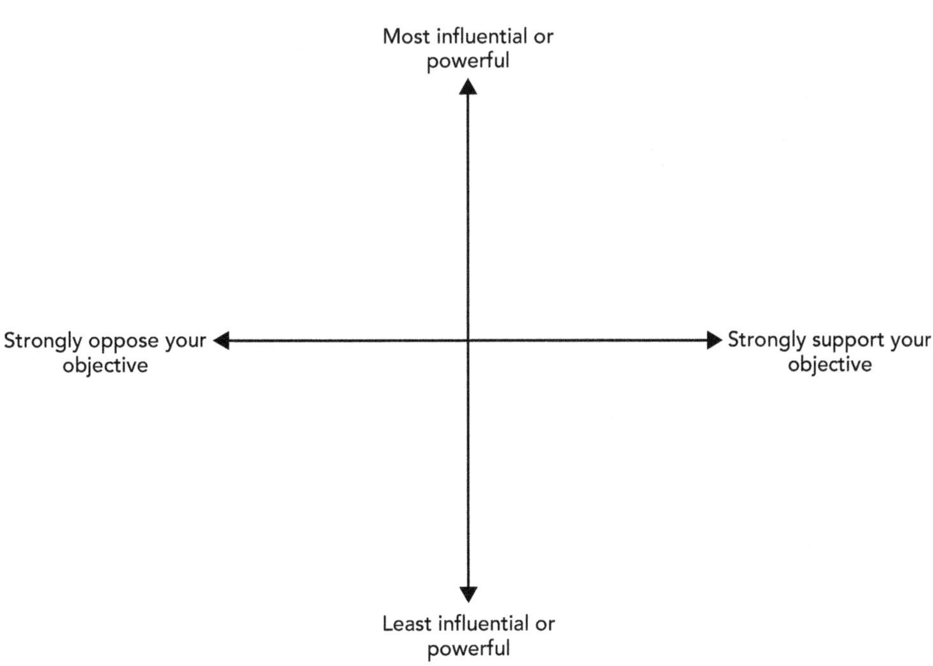

side—if your favorite teacher is also the cousin of the mayor, for example, you might be able to leverage that relationship to get the mayor's attention. Make your best guesses here about these relationships, as they can sometimes be more nuanced or complicated than you think, in preparation for the activity in the next section.

Mapping the Individuals

This step takes the people or organizations identified in the first step and makes them the topic of inquiry: Who are they? What do they care about? What are each individual power player's specific values, interests, pain points, or needs? And, as shown in figure 11.4, how are they connected? When your team knows their audience, they are able to tailor their presentation to the interests of those present. It also helps your team anticipate where there might be bumps—potentially where your policy does not align with

FIGURE 11.4 **Mapping the individuals**

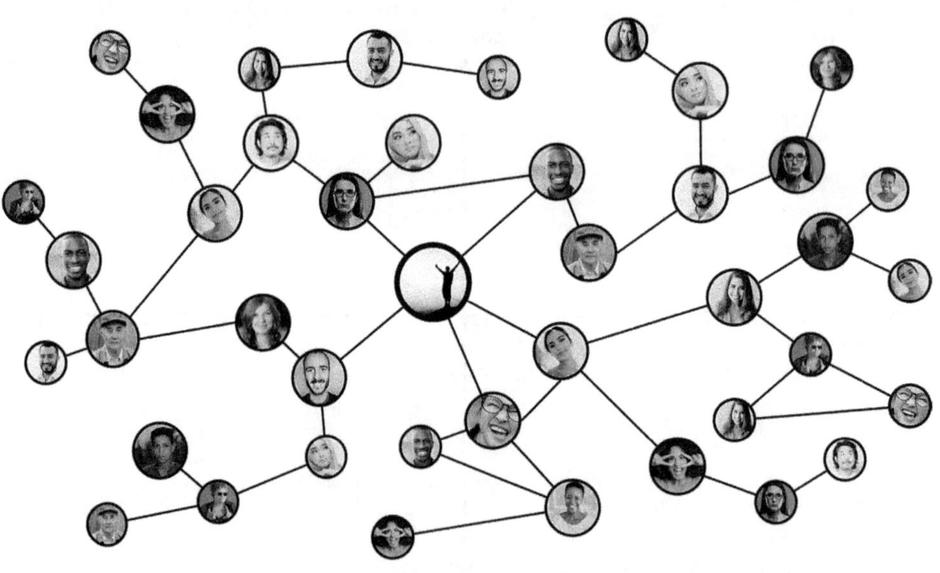

decision-makers' interests—or what types of questions might come from the audience.

If your students are going to a school board meeting or a city council meeting, they can start their research on government websites, identifying who the board members are and which regions they represent. At a student voice competition or presentation, it is helpful to know who the judges are and what organizations they represent. Depending on the size of your team, individuals or groups of students can be assigned to research judges, councillors, or board members. When Dane was a teacher, his middle school writing class wanted a state law adopted that helped undocumented graduates attend college, so they researched the values and life experiences of several on-the-fence legislators. The students conducted dogged research to identify lawmakers sitting on the relevant committees who could help push forward their policy, and they used the information to craft persuasive letters.

In your team's research, they will want to find issues and causes that might be important to these adults: their personal and organizational websites might be helpful, as will social media channels. It can also be helpful to see other organizations with which they might be affiliated. To glean information on the types of questions these adults might ask, look for video of meeting proceedings and notice what questions they have asked in the past. We would recommend compiling this information in a spreadsheet, so your team has notes to share. They can then use these notes to assess where their presentation aligns with the interests of decision-makers and potentially use keywords or examples to speak to said interests. Check the activity box below for an example of this spreadsheet.

Decision-Maker Spreadsheet

NAME	TITLE	ORGANIZATION	EMAIL	SOCIALS	ISSUES OF INTEREST	AFFILIATIONS	POTENTIAL QUESTIONS

Remember that some audience members might not have knowledge or experience with YPAR or student voice. If that is the case, you might need to take time to educate them on these topics.

Uncovering Histories and Contexts

Understanding the history and context of the issue and the power players' relationship to it is important. This connects to root cause analysis, which we focused on in chapter 6. When searching for the roots of a problem, we recommended asking: What are the social, political, and historical origins of the problem? What choices have been made that led to this? Sometimes that is hard to see early in the YPAR process before the youth have conducted research. True to the action research cycle, we recommend constantly pinging back to previous activities to freshen and deepen thinking.

A group of high schoolers and their coach recently had an *aha* moment while engaging in reflection toward the end of their TSV project. After identifying a problem of what they called *achievement pressure* in their high school, the young people named the issue as sort of an implicit or shadow problem in their school. Like the folx Shelley interviewed for her dissertation, the high schoolers said the pressure has always just been there, like it was part of the school. At this point, the coach—a school counselor—perked up. He had just been talking to a few long-time teachers and administrators at the school about its history. Educators who had been there since the beginning of the school's twenty-year history said it had been created specifically to be the gem of the district, to cater to the best of the best. It was built in a fancy neighborhood, and even more affluence followed after the school recorded some of the highest test scores in the state.

The students quickly caught on; one said, "Wait, so you're saying it was built to be this way?" A few other students looked at each other, slack-jawed. They returned to their root cause tree with fresh eyes. The trunk was their problem: the pressure to achieve. The limbs were situations where this pressure popped: AP classes, extracurriculars, pushy parents. The symptoms were their exact lived experiences of the problem—mental health struggles, anxiety, loss of sleep, tension with friends. The roots, which they had murkily defined as "school culture" now became clearer as they considered the historical roots of the problem. The public school was created to be *the best*, and that created heavy pressure on every student who would walk through its doors for decades.

What was painfully obvious to those who had spent their careers at the school proved to be novel understandings for those new to the community. The students now better understood the history of the problem. One said the group had felt stuck earlier, when they were thinking about the historical context, but now they felt excited to look at the problem in new ways. In a group discussion, the students began to wonder if the *school* problem with achievement pressure was actually a *district* problem with school hierarchy and segregation. This shift in their research, which is ongoing as we write, has major implications for their power mapping and next steps—for what they ask for and from whom.

CONCLUSION

So now you have some ideas about the scope of the issues, the policies that are connected, the people who are involved (and what they care about) and the history of the problem. It's time to narrow your focus. Where can you have the most impact, and how are you going to get people to support your cause? One last task to consider: create an impact-effort matrix, where you look at the possibility of building alliances with each person or group and determine the level of impact and the level of effort that will take. (A quick internet search for "impact-effort matrix" shows several examples.) Some alliances are quick and easy to establish, others are harder and take more time. In a perfect world, you will be able to identify low-effort but high-impact activities. Thinking back to the example at the opening of the chapter, it was easy for the Deerfield group to build an alliance with the teachers on the equity council—they had shared goals. And, it was both easy and high impact to create the professional development for teachers and students.

Key Takeaways

- The more you know, the higher the chance of success. Know the people, the system, the policy, and the history.
- People, policies, and practices already exist that can support your work. Take the time to figure out who, what, and how.
- Knowing who opposes you, and why, is as important as knowing your supporters.

Up Next: Building Alliances

Now that you've figured out what you want, who to ask, and what they care about, it's time to build alliances with them to make the change you want to see happen.

FIGURE 11.5 **Power mapping**

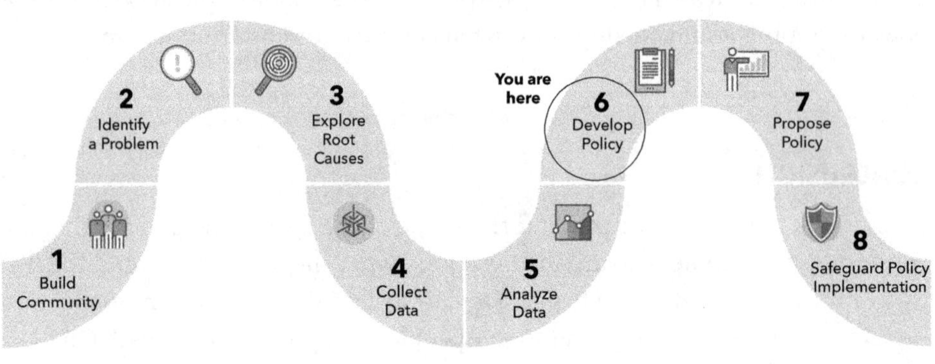

TWELVE

Building Alliances

THE PRIOR CHAPTER INTRODUCED TOOLS for power mapping and understanding the political landscape of the issue you are working on. By now, you should know some of the minefields you may encounter when advocating about this issue. Fortunately, you've also identified a range of potential allies to enlist in your support. Turning those potential allies into real alliances is the purpose of this chapter. We'll take you through tips on how to approach the conversation and who to have it with.

HOW TO BUILD ALLIANCES

Start with Relationships

The building block of political alliances is a one-to-one relationship. Luckily, you and your students already know how to do this. You know how to introduce yourself, ask questions to learn about another person, and do the basic stuff of building relationships. In many of the examples here, you may already have a head start, because you will be talking to colleagues in your building whom you already know. Your students, too, may have a head start by reaching out to peers who lead other groups on campus.

But there are a few elements that community organizers have refined over the years that will help transform this meeting from an initial "get to know you" conversation to a stepping stone to coalition building. Called the *one-to-one* meeting or the *relational* meeting, the core aim of this meeting is to uncover another person's self-interests.

Sometimes people have a negative association with the term *self-interest.* It sounds a lot like selfishness. Isn't *selflessness* a lot better? Don't we want to motivate people based on their desire to help others or their willingness to put aside their own needs? Well . . . those would be nice things to have, but experienced organizers would say no, the most lasting coalitions are those that are based on self-interest. Longtime community organizers Aaron Schutz and Marie Sandy offer a helpful definition in their book, *Collective Action for Social Change*:

> If self-interest isn't selfishness, and it isn't selflessness, what is it?
>
> Self-interests encompass all of those aspects of people that motivate them to act. As Michael Jacoby Brown argues, from an organizing perspective, "self-interest includes our whole selves, our stories and memories and the relationships we have with close friends and family. It involves all that makes us tick and why." Another term that organizers use for self-interest is "passion." When you understand someone's self-interests, you know what makes them angry, what elicits their deep sympathy, and what is likely to generate commitment over the long term. A core self-interest is not simply about what someone wants to get, but about "who" someone is or wants to be.[1]

So as your team aims to build alliances, whether with students, parents, or school personnel, a powerful way to begin is to start to get a sense of a person's passions or self-interests and how those might overlap with your issue. We dug deep into this in chapter 11. Let's say your team is working on an issue like student voice, and you are wanting to see a variety of changes that enable students to have more of a say in their school experience, ranging from classroom culture to school rules. These kinds of changes can be quite threatening to adults. Wouldn't it be wise to enlist at least a few key teachers, especially those who have credibility and respect in the building among other teachers, to show support for your campaign? Adopting some of the practices of a relational meeting might give you some tools to get there. Instead of waiting until the day of a presentation or a public meeting, when teachers are on the spot (and likely to be more defensive), we recommend reaching out to key allies in the weeks or even months leading up to your policy presentation to find common ground. We play out this example below.

Possible questions for a one-to-one meeting:

- What got you into teaching?
- When this school is at its best, what is that like?
- What is the most rewarding thing about this job for you?
- When you're feeling really successful with your classroom teaching, what does that look like?
- What are the biggest challenges you face?

Even a fifteen-minute conversation with another person can generate a great deal of information about what moves them and how they might find common ground with your issue. This part is not easy to forecast in advance; you don't know what they will say. But ideally, as you have these conversations, you start to see ways to make a case. If your team is working on student voice issues, maybe you can convince a teacher that students will be more motivated to learn in their class if they feel more seen and heard. If your team is working on reducing microaggressions by school faculty and leadership, maybe you will find out about an experience your colleague has had where they felt belittled or disrespected and use that to build a bridge of understanding.

EXAMPLE MEETING

You've been on a curriculum committee with the department chair, but you have never really had a conversation about his values or his approach to the work. For the purposes of building alliances, you ask if he'd mind chatting with you for a few minutes during one of your overlapping free periods. Take the opportunity to learn more about him personally: his background, interests, and what motivates him as a person and educator. Maybe he's developed a well-earned cynicism about school reform efforts, so you ask him what first brought him into teaching. You might inquire about what his best experiences have been at the school, or what have been his most satisfying teaching experiences. Now, as he talks to you, you *might* find that his values are completely in opposition to what students want: he's a traditional lecturer, he doesn't understand today's generation, or some such thing. But more likely than not, you'll learn some things about what inspires him that you can use to build support for the student voice initiative. Maybe he tells you that his best experiences have been when students are motivated to learn in class. Or that his favorite years are those where he feels like he has a relationship with his students, with some give and take, rather than just a constant battle to assert his authority. This now provides key information that you can draw on to build his support for greater student voice in the school.

The people you talk to may not always know what their self-interest is, or what their passion is—they may not have had time to think about it in a long time. So the conversation itself is a creative process; in the process of talking, they may begin to see overlapping values in new ways. They may appreciate the respect you've shown by reaching out to try to find common ground. Showing you are good listener goes a long way. You shouldn't try to convince anyone of anything, especially not in your first conversation. Right now, you are listening, trying to understand where they are coming from, and using that info to build a sense of trust that can be built on as your team continues its work.

WHOM TO BUILD ALLIANCES WITH

At Your School

In chapter 11, we emphasized the importance of getting crystal clear on your issue and your proposed solution; this clarity will help you recruit allies as you seek political support. Think about all the other student groups or stakeholders in your school and how the issue you are working on might impact or be of interest to them. Is there a GSA (gender/sexuality alliance), or an affinity group, like a Black student union? What about a social justice or multicultural club?

A good example of this can be seen in work the students did in Deerfield to map out who the power players were at their school, as we discussed in chapter 11. Students who wanted to raise awareness about microaggressions found out who the key players were and where there were opportunities for collaboration. A key part of their success was enlisting support from teachers whose interests overlapped with theirs about the issue.

If you're lucky, you might have a school principal who is supportive of student voice or the specific issue your students are working on. In this case, nurturing a relationship with the principal early on can be beneficial, especially if they do not try to micromanage or take over the project. We have seen examples where the principal or assistant principal made a point to visit the TSV class once a month to find out about progress on the project, ask questions, and give feedback. In one case, this worked really well, in part because all parties had a similar goal: to reduce bullying in the school. Students felt seen; their project was "real" and not just a school exercise. Just as important, the school leadership had a sense of where the work was headed and could think about how to align top-down efforts with student-led efforts. Having an open door like this also helps students get feedback about which strategies are most likely to be impactful or be implemented, and which ones might be dead ends. There is a risk here, though, which is that a school leader might use the relationship to try to short-circuit the process or place boundaries on the more radical dreams of students. Watch out for that. But because you are working in a system where principals have a lot of power, the more you can have access to this person, the more likely you are to see results.

Outside of Your School

Community organizations and activists

Some projects may call for alliances with community organizations or parent groups outside of your school. In Colorado, for example, we have worked with several schools where students focused on improving the quality of school lunches. One group connected with a nonprofit organization in the Denver area whose mission was to provide high-quality, healthy, affordable school lunches. By developing a relationship and learning what the cost would be to the school, the student group was able to approach the school principal with an informed proposal about what it would take to bring in the organization as a partner.

We have also seen TSV teams connect with community organizing groups that share a similar vision. In 2020, for example, a team of high school students had been working on a yearlong project focused on disrupting the school-to-prison pipeline by limiting roles for police in schools; this was part of a national police-free schools movement that caught on across the US during the summer of racial reckoning. It just so happened that an outside parent organizing group had been coalescing on that issue during the previous decade. The students and the organization joined forces, found allies on the district school board, and created a powerful coalition that succeeded in banning police from city schools.

In rare cases, you may work in a school where there are existing chapters or student clubs run by an independent community organization. In Philadelphia, for example, there is a group called City Students United (CSU) that operates inside of the schools but also independently of them. Teachers act as sponsors for chapters so that CSU clubs can meet at the school, but paid community organizers from CSU typically lead the chapter, recruit students, and facilitate student activities. Hypothetically, because of their experience with political activism and connections to other youth organizations, an outside community organizing group could be a powerful ally for work that your students do. But it's important for you to recognize that you are operating under different constraints and pressures. The organizers are *outsiders*: they are paid by their community organization, not the school district, and they are motivated by a vision of holding the district accountable for educational justice and student voice. They most likely don't have a formal relationship with the district as a whole, but instead try to create relationships with teachers. But teachers and administrators are accountable to school and district rules, and they risk sanctions (possibly as serious as job loss) if activism campaigns step too far outside the lines of school or district policies.

At Oak Knoll High School, a series of racialized incidents were not resolved in ways that were transparent or meaningful to the Black student population. In frustration that their voices were not being heard, the students reached out to a community activist who was not affiliated with the district to help them strategize. Each day for a week, the students walked out of class and convened in a local park. The activist assisted them in organizing (and publicizing) the walkouts, which brought the attention of the local news media and the broader community. In this sense, the alliance was successful in increasing awareness about the issue. The downside, however, was that the outsider status of the activist enabled the district to be dismissive of what they characterized as a nonsanctioned walkout planned by an unaffiliated activist.

These examples show that creating an alliance, even temporary, with community organizations brings potential benefits and risks. Benefits stem when there is close alignment with the values and agenda of the community organization and when the organization brings a power base as representatives of the community. Risks stem from the different institutional and political contexts faced by activists: they are not employees of the district; their job is to hold schools and districts to account. As a teacher or school leader, you operate in a narrower context. The best alliances are those where all parties recognize this and find ways to work together that honors the fact that school personnel may need to limit how they communicate or advocate in the public sphere.

Using social media or legacy media

Sometimes students will want to promote their views on social media or through reaching out to local TV news. One such example, which Dane has written about, took place when students were fired up in support of their teachers who had just gone on strike. The use of social media brought new attention to student voice and to the student activists in particular; one of the students was contacted by a national magazine and recruited by national political parties. This brought some attention, but much of it was unwanted, as the student faced backlash from her school administration and local actors. So there are risks.

The same goes for legacy media, such as TV news. We remember a schoolteacher whose class was working on a project to call attention to the lack of spaces to play or exercise at their school. They did not have a gym and ran track in the school hallways. The students reached out to a range of local media outlets and ultimately drew the attention of a local television station, which aired a story. Although this had the benefit of drawing attention to the issue, here, too, there was a negative backlash from the school leaders and administration. They did not like being caught flat-footed by a negative story about their school. The teacher faced criticism from the school leadership. Fortunately, they saw her strengths as a teacher, and she was not penalized for her action.

ALLIANCES ARE NECESSARY, BUT COMPLICATED

School leaders make their decisions in a specific and highly constrained ecosystem. If your team is making policy recommendations or calling for programs that may challenge the status quo, antagonize key stakeholders (such as veteran teachers), or require shifts in the budget, then you will need more than just well-reasoned arguments. Nine times out of ten, having data to support your point will be valuable but ultimately insufficient for moving decision-makers to act. You also need power.

We know that students and teachers don't have much positional authority or formal power when it comes to most American public schools. But you do have power in numbers. And you can expand your power by building key alliances, whether inside of your building, such as with other student groups or key teachers, or outside of your building, with community organizations, nonprofit groups, or parents. This chapter has shared examples that, we hope, provide specific ideas for how you might build those alliances. As you do that, however, we want you to be mindful of the risks.

Consider the Risks

Risk one: exposure to backlash

This is when stuff gets real. Advocating for change, and building a political voice that can't be dismissed or treated as a cute exercise, will provoke defensiveness by some people. The more you push, the more you should be ready for backlash. Students are not immune: they might be called reckless, they might be scapegoated by teachers, or they might be the objects of efforts to manipulate or scare them. Similarly, you, the teacher, may face backlash, including from colleagues who disagree or school leaders who don't like what you're up to. Adults who don't like what your students are saying will accuse you of manipulating, indoctrinating, or brainwashing your students. We have seen it all.

If you are going to lean into supporting your students in their action research, you can't eliminate this risk. Instead, we advise you to try to make the risk as visible as possible, for all parties, and then make an informed decision. So, for example, if your students want to organize a walkout without getting permission from the principal, they should think through what the consequences might be. If they want to put their principal on blast on social media, you should similarly help them weigh the pros and cons. Don't hesitate to tell them what your limits are, or how their actions could affect your well-being and livelihood. Students will be sensitive to that.

Ultimately, you, as the teacher, need to check on yourself and decide what your boundaries are and where you are comfortable taking risk. You are not expected to facilitate a project that puts your job in jeopardy. We're not asking for martyrs. Instead, we ask you to try to map out what the consequences and risks are, be open about it, talk about it with your students (and allies who are teachers), and move from there. That conversation alone will be a rich learning opportunity for everyone.

Risk two: conflicts between outsider and insider strategies

As suggested in the discussion of City Students United, grassroots community organizers often have different tactics and more radical politics than people working within schools. Outsiders who take activist positions do not risk losing their jobs; in fact, they are more likely *fulfilling* their jobs by pushing as hard as they can on district leaders. Insiders navigate a different institutional system, with its own rewards and punishments. Insiders are often necessary, because they have the power to implement the kinds of policy changes that outsiders want to see. The effort to build an alliance among actors from both sides is not easy. Outsiders may want to push harder than is wise for insiders. So be vigilant about this and try to talk openly about it as you forge the coalition. You will be stronger if the alliance is strong, but the alliance needs to create room for action by all parties.

CONCLUSION

Key Takeaways

- Encourage your students to develop alliances with other student clubs or school stakeholders.
- You can support your students by seeking common ground with key adults in your building.
- Alliances with outside community organizers can help your team build its power and impact, but they come with risks. Know your limits and boundaries.

Up Next: Presenting Compelling Arguments

Now that you've mapped out power brokers in your school and developed some level of coalition or alliance with those key players, it's time to get ready to present your arguments in the public sphere. In the next chapter we share tips for how to support your students in developing high-quality presentations and policy arguments.

FIGURE 12.1 **Building alliances**

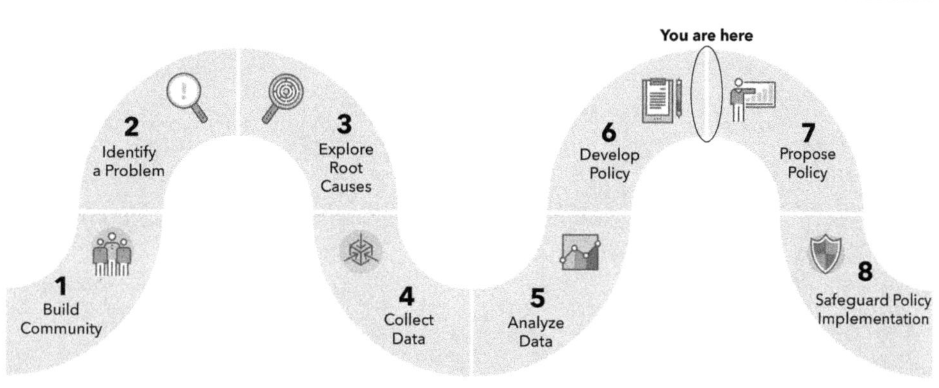

THIRTEEN

Presenting Compelling Policy Arguments

YOU AND YOUR STUDENTS have put in a lot of work to get to this point. You've debated the issue; you've gathered evidence; you've honed your social change strategy. Now it's time to make a compelling call to action for a public audience. Don't cut corners now. You might feel like the hard work is behind you, but it is crucial to prepare for this time when you have the attention of key decision-makers or stakeholders. Be creative in your approach. Catch and hold their attention. Be prepared for questions and challenges. Practice! The purpose of this chapter is to help your class honor its work by having a smart change strategy and communicating it in a compelling way.

NAIL YOUR OPENING

At student voice competitions and in public testimony, judges or decision-makers will hear from countless people, and presentations can get monotonous. Your group wants to leave an impression. A good opening hook will make your group stand out and set the tone for your presentation.

A hook is a presentation technique that grabs the attention of your audience. A good hook also serves as a throughline for your presentation. It establishes your point right away, reemerges throughout the presentation (helping to hold the presentation together), and drives home your conclusion. As such, your hook should not be random. It is a purposeful tool to help you make your policy argument. You want your hook to be impactful, but it cannot be long—thirty seconds to a minute, tops.

A good hook should be clever and creative. Some of the best hooks we have seen have used poetry, video, or brief skits. The presenters were animated and delivered their hook with a passion that drew in the audience. Other groups have used quick polls to ask the audience's opinion, inviting the audience to participate while introducing the presentation topic in fun ways.

In designing your hook, help students think back to the experience of identifying the topic. Was there an *aha* moment along the way? Or something else that inspired your group to pursue this line of inquiry? If so, use this as a source of inspiration for your hook.

Mine the talent of your student group. Do you have a poet who wants to try their hand at writing something? How about an artist who is willing to draw a representation of your team's work? Invite your team to harness their talents.

Possibly one of the most creative opening hooks we have seen was from Fresh DC, described in the box below. Through the rest of the chapter, we will return to Fresh DC's whole presentation as an anchor example to ground our recommendations. Some elements of Fresh DC's presentation were exemplary; we also point out ways it could have been improved.

Fresh DC's Opening Hook

Fresh DC was a student voice group from a school in Washington, DC. As part of a national competition on youth voice, these young people were advocating for tasty and healthy lunch options at their school.

For their opening hook, the youth took the stage to the music of a popular pop song. Each young person danced their way to the stage. One young man took to the microphone and rapped, changing the words of the original song to align with the theme of their presentation: "We're bringing healthy back. Unhealthy foods are really wack."

NAME THE PROBLEM

Most youth voice work centers on youth addressing an issue that impacts their school or community. For simplicity's sake, we call this *the problem*. It is the thing that young people are seeking to call attention to or address though research and policymaking.

The challenge can come from the complexity of some problems. As a result, youth might be tempted to list off the various issues related to their problem. Let's return to the example from Fresh DC.

Fresh DC Names the Problem

After finishing their opening hook, and to help make their argument for the need for tasty and healthy foods at schools, the youth asked the audience what they thought of their school lunches growing up. They also shared a slide with how students at their school described their school lunch: "nasty" and "gross." To contextualize the need for healthy school lunches, the team then described the Anacostia area of DC as a food desert, and they shared information on food-related health disparities in the District.

While all the factors that Fresh DC listed definitely impact the need for healthy lunches, describing them in the manner that they did could confuse the audience. What problem are they addressing—is it unhealthy lunches, food deserts in DC, or health disparities? What larger social issue are they connecting to? This might cause adult decision-makers to question the focus of the presentation and ultimately hurt a team's ability to have their message heard.

In naming your problem, it is therefore important to clearly state the issue you will address. Quite literally saying, "The problem we seek to address is the need for healthy lunches in schools," for example. You will want to be as explicit as possible with your audience throughout your presentation.

Contextualize the Problem

There are several reasons to give some context to your problem. One is to show you have done your homework; you have put in the time to research the issue you seek to address. Addressing the context of your problem might also be necessary to educate your audience. In some cases, they might only know the symptoms of the issue and not the deeper underlying concerns. It also gives you the opportunity to highlight both the prevalence of the issue and how it is impacting youth.

Perhaps most importantly, your contextual analysis of the problem should relate to how you design your solution. If your analysis of the problem just focuses on symptoms, then the remedy might be just as superficial. For example, you might succeed in replacing sugary beverages with club soda, but then no one buys the club soda. In describing your context, go back to your team's root cause analysis. What was a key factor that impacts your problem? To provide context, your team can also consider how the issue manifests and how it impacts youth.

Make the Problem Relevant

We have found that adult decision-makers are more apt to listen to young people when the young people describe how a problem impacts them. Sharing how you are impacted by the problem makes the issue personal. It is harder to dismiss the concerns of youth when faced by those who are affected by the problem. In essence you are helping put a face to the problem.

We discussed this a bit in chapter 8 when talking about qualitative research, but some student voice teams are hesitant to inject their experience into their presentation. Perhaps this goes back to the overemphasis on being objective about research. In this case, when making a policy proposal, the ability to name your connection to the problem is an asset that gives credibility to your argument and can inject passion into your presentation.

RESEARCH METHODS

Fresh DC Shows Their Methods

To prove the viability of their tasty and healthy lunch program, the youth from Fresh DC carried out a series of taste tests. The young people prepared two healthy food options and shared them with their schoolmates.

In their presentation, Fresh DC shared data on their schoolmates' opinions of the food options. They used two pie charts to demonstrate to the audience how the majority of their schoolmates either liked or loved the new food options. They then played a couple of video testimonials from students describing why they preferred the healthy food options.

Describe Your Methods

As part of your student voice presentation, it is important to clearly describe the research methods your team employed. Did your team do surveys, interviews, archival research, or literature reviews? Describing this clearly grounds the audience in the type of data they should expect to hear. This was something Fresh DC did well. They clearly described their taste test and post-taste test survey.

It is also important to describe the quantity and type of data you obtained. If you have done a really robust job on your research, sharing this will win you some credibility with decision-makers. This is an area where Fresh DC did not do such a great job. They never addressed how many students participated in the taste test. Although most of their respondents enjoyed the healthy food options, there is a big difference between ten students really liking the food or two hundred students. Similarly, if you are doing archival research or a literature review, how many artifacts were reviewed, and where did you do your search? By addressing this clearly you are again demonstrating the thoroughness of your team's work and advancing your credibility.

Connect Your Methods to the Problem or Policy

As we stated earlier in the chapter, a great policy presentation has a throughline. The hook, the research, and the policy are all clearly related, with each section building toward the next. It is therefore important that you help the audience understand how your research methods are related to the problem you seek to address or the policy you will propose.

This does not need to be extensive or elaborate, but was something that Fresh DC unfortunately skipped over. It would have been sufficient for them to say, "We conducted taste tests in order to demonstrate that youth enjoy healthy food options."

You might think that the reasons for selecting a particular research method are self-evident, but we recommend that you do not leave this to chance. As the presenter, you control the narrative; communicating your rationale directly to your audience leaves less room for them to have to fill in the blanks or to develop doubts.

Present Your Findings

A challenge in any public comment or youth voice presentation is getting all the elements of your presentation addressed within a limited time block. This gets further complicated when you conduct a research study and likely have a plethora of data. Maybe there are frequencies and means, participant quotes, or pictures. Here it is important to present the data that best supports your case in a manner that is efficient and speaks to your audience.

We have discussed part of this in earlier chapters, but start by identifying key pieces of data that support your argument, that address the prevalence or severity of your problem, or that support the efficacy of your policy proposal. In the case of Fresh DC, they wanted to demonstrate that young people would eat healthy food options, so presenting statistics and video testimonials of youth endorsing the healthy food options made sense. They kept it simple, sharing the percentage of students who liked or loved the new food options.

Next, consider how you are presenting your results. Rattling off statistics, even if they support your argument, might get boring. As we described in earlier chapters, using visuals like bar graphs and pie charts can make data easier to understand. This was what Fresh DC did, using pie charts that showed the percentage of students who liked and loved their food.

Things can get a little trickier with qualitative or archival methods. Though you want to address the general themes of your findings, you also want to provide evidence to highlight what your themes mean. This is where selecting a few quotes or key images is helpful. We have talked earlier about deriving qualitative findings; here it is more about incorporating them into your presentation in an effective manner. Fresh DC used video testimonials to help convey their qualitative data. What was nice about this was that not only did the testimonials help make their case, the animated nature of one testimonial injected humor and energy into their presentation.

One challenge with quotes, whether written, audio, or video, is ensuring that you do not put participants at risk. We have seen examples of adult administrators enacting retribution on students for being vocally critical of schools. It is good practice to get permission from the participant and to only share the elements of the quote that are essential to make your point, while shielding the participant's identity.

THE POLICY PROPOSAL AND CALL TO ACTION

Your team's presentation is all leading up to a specific call to action. This is not just an academic exercise or a science fair. Your students have worked long and hard because this issue affects them directly, and they want to see it changed. There are two areas to focus on when working with students: the proposal itself and the specific actions you are calling for from your audience.

The Policy Proposal

Any problem has multiple possible solutions or change strategies. Take Fresh DC's topic of unhealthy food. Some students might want to focus on the school lunches and persuade the district or school to change vendors or introduce new options. Still others might think education and public awareness is needed, and they might call for a teach-in on consuming healthy food or paint a mural depicting urban gardens on the side of the school. Some categories of options are shown in table 13.1.

Within our TSV group, we tend to favor change strategies that get at root causes. Often, identifying a policy that can change is the key way to do that. Policies are different from service projects or educational workshops. Policies are a way to create rules or laws that then change how institutions such as schools work. Once you get a school leader to agree to a policy, you can hold them accountable for implementing that policy. Policies are meant to continue from year to year because they are written into the budget or into a set of rules or commitments. Table 13.2 shares examples of local, state, and national policies.

After students brainstorm possible policies to address their issue, we recommend identifying the top two or three ideas and then evaluating them in relation to the following questions:

TABLE 13.1 Change strategies (using healthy food as the example)

TYPES OF CHANGE	EXAMPLE	PROS	CONS
Education / Public awareness	Stage a teach-in or an assembly; paint a mural	Within your control (your team could execute this plan, and it does not require a major lift from administrators)	One-off (may not lead to sustained change)
Community service	Organize a food drive or invite donations for the cafeteria	Within your control	One-off (may not lead to sustained change)
Policy change	Change school vendors	Leads to a tangible change in food options	Complex, may take several years, and is dependent on many factors, including budgets, district procurement policies, etc.

TABLE 13.2 Examples of policies

PROBLEM	LEVEL	SAMPLE POLICY CHANGE
Parents who are native Spanish speakers do not feel welcome in the school	School	School administrators agree to adopt a policy that all materials sent to parents will be offered in Spanish and English, and that they will allocate resources in the budget to pay for translation or hire a bilingual liaison using Title funds.
Too many fast-food restaurants and not enough healthy food	City	City government agrees to create tax incentives for grocery stores to sell fresh produce in a specific zip code.
Undocumented students cannot afford out-of-state tuition rates	State	The state legislature passes a law that Colorado residents who attended Colorado high schools for four years are eligible for in-state tuition.

- *Is it clear and specific?* The proposal names a set of rules or laws, identifies who is responsible for implementing them, and specifies a timeline for implementation.
- *Does it address root causes?* The policy proposal may not fix everything about the problem, but it is more than a Band-Aid; it addresses the causes of the problem for as many people as possible at your school or neighborhood.
- *Will it continue after you graduate?* The policy is not a onetime thing; it is set into rules so that future students and teachers will experience the benefits.
- *Is it supported by evidence?* You've done research that supports the policy or shows why it is important.
- *Does it promote justice and fairness?* The policy is meant to be inclusive of all people and ensure that everyone has access to opportunity; it either corrects past injustices or ensures that it does not just benefit the already privileged.

After going through your policy ideas and discussing their pros and cons against these questions, you might arrive at consensus in the class about where to focus. But more likely than not, this will be a key time to test your decision-making practices as a group. (See chapters 2 and 5 for group decision-making strategies.) It may take several class periods to arrive at a clear policy proposal that your team can get behind with passion and conviction.

The Call to Action

Just as important as the substance of your proposal is the need to think carefully about the call to action you will make to your audience. In the power mapping phase (discussed in chapter 11) you will have identified who the key players are for your topic and who you need to convince. You might think of these people as your targets. Now is the time to hit them with the most convincing and powerful message you can.

The first strategy is to know your audience and have a sense of the values that move them. You might explore ways to frame your issue for this audience that will be true to your values while also bridging to the values of the audience. For example, there is a scene in the movie *Footloose* where the protagonist wants to convince the town elders to allow the teenagers to hold a dance. Knowing that the elders are motivated by religious beliefs, the protagonist finds a biblical quotation (from Ecclesiastes) that praises dance, thus undermining their core argument. Similarly, some young immigration activists were famously effective at winning over skeptical audiences by positioning their desire for a path to citizenship along the lines of shared values and interests with politicians. One of the authors of this book, Dane, encouraged his students to research the webpages of each state legislator in order to discern what kind of persuasive argument would move them to vote for the Colorado ASSET bill, which was intended to make undocumented students eligible for in-state tuition at public universities.

Strategy number two is to back up effective framing and use of evidence with *power in numbers*. Sometimes decision-makers are moved more by political pressure than anything else. Can your students invite parents to the meeting? Can they invite community coalitions or community allies? Look back to chapter 12 for tips on how to build a coalition that makes it harder for decision-makers to dismiss or ignore your arguments.

Our final strategy is to offer a clear timeline and accountability measures for decision-makers. Who is responsible for enacting your policy proposal? If they are not in the audience, what can your audience do to prod them into action? When do you expect results? On what date will you be following up with decision-makers for a progress report? What does success look like in one month, six months, and one year? Unfortunately, if you have a terrific policy but no clear and public form of accountability, it is easy for decision-makers to bide their time and make promises with no intent to follow through. This speaks to a long-term change strategy that is important to think about; few policy wins happen in one semester or year. This may be an issue that subsequent groups of students need to pick up. We speak to this more in chapter 16, which explores how to ensure continuity in projects while working with new groups of students.

CONCLUSION

Key Takeaways

- *Nail your opening.* Have something that is clever and creative and that draws the audience's attention.
- *Clearly name the problem you seek to address.* Provide some context for the importance of your problem and how it relates to your students' experience.
- *Describe your research methods.* Connect them to your focal problem. Deliver results in a way that highlights key outcomes.
- *Have a clear policy proposal.* The point is to impact change. Make sure your proposal addresses your presenting concern. Use your call to action to solicit support. Have a timeline for policy implementation.
- *Be prepared for audience questions.* There may well be questions that seek to discredit or belittle the youth. Role-playing can be a good way to practice your responses. (There will be more on this in the next chapter.)

Up Next: Speaking Truth to Power

Presenting policy arguments, as complex as it is, is pretty straightforward. What happens when the adult audience members are unresponsive or even hostile toward youth? Chapter 14 examines the challenges of youth speaking truth to power.

FIGURE 13.1 **Presenting the project**

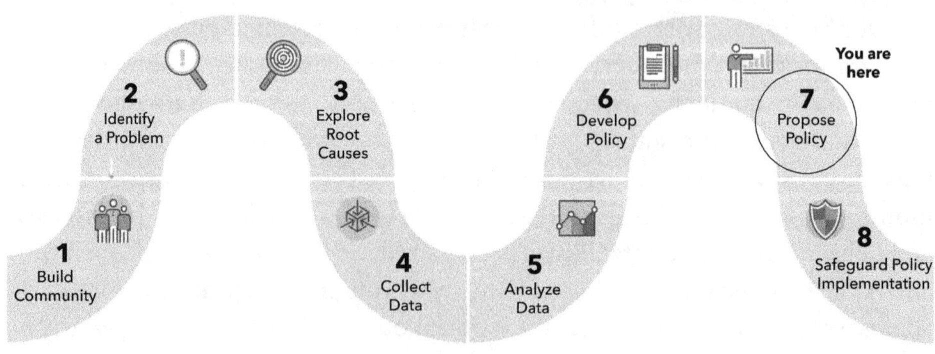

FOURTEEN

Speaking Truth to Power

with Bea Salazar

IN CHAPTER 4, WE INTRODUCED YOU to the action civics team from John Lewis High School (JLHS). As you might remember, they were interested in issues of school safety. As the students progressed through the TSV cycle, they learned that their school district was in the process of reexamining the districtwide safety plan. The youth felt that student voice was essential in reformulating this plan and that students should be represented on the planning committee. Therefore, at a district event, the leaders of the JLHS action civics team decided to approach the superintendent to learn more about the process for reformulating the district safety plan and to ask for student representation on this committee.

Two JLHS students approached the superintendent, introduced themselves, and stated their purpose to learn more about the revised safety plan. The superintendent was caught a little off guard. He mentioned he would need to look into when that process would take place, but he did offer to follow up via email. The youth pressed him, though; they knew the committee had already begun meeting. They then asked for student representatives to be placed on the committee. Though the interaction remained professional, the youth were assertive.

The next day, the action civics team at JLHS was scolded by their principal, who had received an angry email from the superintendent accusing the students of harassing him and behaving inappropriately at the event. The student leader of the JLHS team consulted with a trusted adult ally and, based on that adult's recommendation, reached out to the superintendent to request a meeting to further discuss the district safety plan.

Speaking truth to power is never easy, but it can be particularly challenging for youth in adult-led spaces. As we saw in the above case, adults are not used to being questioned by young people. This puts additional pressure on youth voice teams to consider their tactics when they enter adult spaces. Youth must prepare for adults who might dismiss them, ask tough questions, or display hostility. In the previous chapter, we walked through the nuts and bolts of good policy presentations. This chapter is about more than presentations. In this chapter, we discuss how adult facilitators can help prepare youth to make their demands heard. We begin by addressing adult behaviors that might impede student voice (such as adultism and discourse of surprise). We then provide some suggested activities to help youth prepare to speak their truths.

ADULT RESPONSES TO YOUTH RESEARCH

Adultism and the discourse of surprise are two of the most common forms of adult behaviors we have observed that impede student voice progress. Adultism has been defined as a set of beliefs and attitudes that adults are superior to and, as a result, are entitled to make decisions on behalf of youth.[1] Adultism can manifest in interpersonal interactions, such as indifference toward youth, tokenization, and mistreatment, as well as through institutional policies and curriculum.[2] Specifically in student voice work, the concerns of youth are often not taken as seriously as those of the adults, nor are youth seen as worthy of adult respect.[3] Also within the spectrum of adultism is what Melanie Bertrand calls the "discourse of surprise."[4] This is an expression of disbelief and amazement that youth have engaged in a Youth Participatory Action Research (YPAR) process or other form of student voice that seeks to bring meaningful change to the school or school district. Though expressed as praise or astonishment, discourse of surprise takes attention away from the messages of youth and instead communicates adults' disbelief over what young people are capable of; in other words, a form of gaslighting.

Adults can also unknowingly impede the potential of student voice by their limited knowledge of YPAR. Ben and his colleagues found that when adults were asked about how YPAR has impacted policies and decisions at the school or district level, many responses demonstrated that administrators and decision-makers did not understand what YPAR was.[5] Most decision-makers and administrators thought of YPAR projects as student councils meant to provide direct feedback to administrators or other, even less meaningful forms of student engagement, such as organizing social events for their peers. Adults interviewed also thought of YPAR as responses to surveys led and administered by the school district. When the YPAR projects were seen as research projects, administrators often sought to discredit the research through questions of reliability, reproducibility, and objectivity, and they overlooked the demands of YPAR.

Despite many of the negative responses to YPAR, Ben found that administrators and staff were often quite interested in learning more about the power of the lived experiences of their students.[6] For many of the administrators, hearing stories from the students in their schools often helped them better understand the everyday lives of the students they are meant to serve. Helping administrators understand the importance of youth voice in policy proposals can be just as important as explaining the research that was conducted.

PREPARING TO SPEAK TRUTH

Something we have seen in our youth voice work is that a youth team and their adult facilitator will spend months on analyzing root causes, conducting research, identifying findings, and developing a policy proposal. But then they only spend a few days on their presentations to stakeholders. This robs youth of the opportunity to craft their policy arguments in a way that appeals to adult decision-makers. It also leaves limited time to prepare youth for how they will deal with questions and pushback from their audience. The goal of this section is to provide some suggested activities for preparing to engage with difficult adult audiences.

Acknowledge the Challenge

As is evident from some of the research we wrote about above, sometimes adults can be jerks. As the facilitator of a youth voice group, it is best to acknowledge this. Tell youth that some adults might question their knowledge or offer faint praise for their efforts. Having these conversations in advance is a way to prepare your youth for the challenges they will face.

Carlos calls this approach to working with adults *pessimistic optimism*: when you expect the worst, only better things can happen. As such, your team will likely need to overprepare. Know your policy and your research and try to anticipate the questions that will come from your audience. We will share more about how to do this in the subsequent subsections.

SCIENCE TECH CHARTER EXAMPLE

The student voice team at Science Tech Charter (STC) was preparing for a districtwide youth policy competition. Ahmed, the student leader of the team, assigned each team member a section of their presentation. In addition, team members were assigned responsibility for answering certain types of questions. One student would answer questions about the teams' research methods, another about their policy proposal, and so on.

The team had practiced their presentation with some school leaders and community members. These adults provided them with feedback on how to improve for their final presentation and gave them an idea of the types of questions they might get during the competition. The students practiced responding to questions that came up during these trial runs. Ahmed gave his team members feedback on how to improve on their responses to adult questions.

Finally, the team did some research on the judge panel for the competition, looking for their areas of interest and trying to anticipate what types of questions they would ask. Ahmed recognized the name of one specific judge. He told the team that this judge had asked hard questions at a previous event, and they would have to bring their A game if they were to win over that judge.

Know Your Audience

If you haven't read chapter 11 yet, demerit. We advise that you go back and read about power mapping right now before proceeding further. Even if you have read it, maybe return to it; understanding your audience is necessary when attempting to speak truth to power.

Practice, Practice, Practice

Most policy presentations, which we explored in depth in the previous chapter, will leave time for questions or comments from your target audience. Some questions will focus on clarifying evidence or details of the proposal. Some responses will challenge the accuracy of student claims or the viability of their proposal.

And, sadly, some responses will ignore the focus of the presentation altogether. We still remember the moment when, after a team of students asked for school board members' questions about their proposal to improve their school facilities, all they got was, "How'd you get so cool?"

Fortunately, there are lots of ways to prepare for questions so that your students are ready to react in the situation. Some educators call this *adaptive expertise* because it shows the ability to depart from their prerehearsed scripts and really get into dialogue and interaction with the audience. One effective strategy is to role-play scenarios in which youth practice their responses to hostile or skeptical questions or comments. This can be really fun, and you, the teacher, get to play the target audience. When Ben does this, he'll sometimes be condescending, sometimes hostile, and sometimes ask thoughtful questions. He wants the presenters to be ready for anything. We like the approach that STC took, assigning team members responsibility for particular types of questions. It is hard to know all aspects of a project; this way a team member can focus their efforts on knowing a certain area. As a team, you must prepare for questions that have adultist tones, that are discrediting, and that demonstrate discourse of surprise (see the box on the next page for some common questions we have seen adults ask). Role-play how these questions will be asked and how you will respond. Even if adults are complete jerks, seldom is it helpful to take an adversarial tone. So when practicing, work not only on the *content* of the response but also on your word choice and the *tone* of your response.

In another preparatory approach, one group we observed trained its youth to "caucus" with each other if a meeting was going in a direction they did not expect. Caucusing enables youth to pause the meeting, leave the room, confer with one another, and then return with a shared response. We have observed in some cases that youth have such limited expectations for their interactions with adults that if the adults are polite, the meeting feels like a success. We advise groups to expect more from adults, including demanding that adult policymakers spell out how and when they will follow through on the particular issues raised. Pushing decision-makers in this way will often lead to deeper discussions that involve improvisation and deliberation.

We may be sounding like Allen Iverson, talking about *practice* all the time, but the opportunity to run through both your presentation and how you will answer questions can help your team tremendously. The team at STC did a couple of practice runs of their presentation with school and community leaders. Another educator has her team practice monthly with a rotating audience of school leaders and teachers. Initially these meetings are to help the youth talk out their ideas pertaining to problem identification and root cause analysis. In the second half of the year, as the youth begin fleshing out their presentation, the shared time becomes more about gaining feedback on their policy, policy argument, and the types of questions they should anticipate from district leaders. To the degree you can, give your team the opportunity to practice.

There is an important caveat with practice though: you want to invite adult partners who can be *critical friends*, who will give the youth honest feedback and provide critique that is aimed at helping the team improve. You don't want gold stars for effort; you want adult partners who will help your team get better and help them anticipate the pushback they might face. There is a myth that youth are fragile, but as can be seen in the case above, they can use critique to help them prepare. Carlos happened to be observing STC as they prepared for their presentation and knew the judge they were talking about. Carlos sent the judge a text to let him know that his feedback was helping the team prepare. The judge relayed a message to the youth wishing them luck and praising them for their work thus far. The youth at STC appreciated this recognition.

TYPICAL QUESTIONS OR FEEDBACK

- What made you choose *this* problem?
- Why *these* research methods?
- How do we know your results are not biased?
- Why not focus your proposal on x, y, or z instead?
- How much will this program cost? How will this policy be funded?
- What type of pushback have you seen or do you anticipate?
- Which other decision-makers have you met with, and what have they said?
- What exactly would you like me and the board to do with this information?
- Why are you so cute?
- Wow, it is so cool that you did all this hard work.
- Are you sure someone else didn't write this for you?

Build Contingent Authority

To gain authority in adult decision-making spheres—and as a preemptive strategy against doubt—youth need to build their reputation and competence.[7] In the STC example, students used district bylaws to show that their change proposals were consistent with the district's own rules for how it was supposed to be governed. There are a number of strategies to this end; one approach is who your team aligns itself with. The support and presence of influential policymakers and university faculty can lend legitimacy to your team's policy proposal.[8] Invite your allies to attend your presentation and consider shouting them out during your presentation.

Remind your youth that they are the experts of their experience, data, and policy. Encourage them to approach their presentation as the experts that they are; projecting confidence and authority can diffuse doubts in your audience. We have seen adults try to diminish research findings by asking hypotheticals or attempting to inject hypotheses unrelated to the questions a team sought to answer. Remembering that they are the experts of the data, help youth team members to bring the focus back to what their results demonstrated.

The Aftermath

After the presentation, it is important to process the experience the youth just went through. Emotions, whether of elation or disappointment, are an important factor for educators to manage and support. While it might be easiest to start off with all that went wrong, we encourage you to begin with what went well. It is important to recognize what went well in order to reinforce that for next time. There isn't anything that is too small to be listed here. The more you reinforce what went well, the easier it will be to build from that. On the other hand, recognizing, making space, and troubleshooting the things that did not go well is also an important part of the process. Questions for this phase can look like:

- What are some of the things that went well? What did we do to prepare to help those pieces be successful?
- What are areas that we could have better prepared for? What could we have done differently?

Remember, there are pieces that are completely out of your control, such as other people's reactions, but actively preparing for those can help support youth to respond. After the initial processing has been completed, talk about next steps:

- What needs to be done in order to move forward?
- Who do we need to follow up with?
- What are our next steps?

CONCLUSION

Key Takeaways

- Adultism and discourse of surprise are ways in which adults derail student voice efforts.
- Prepare by having honest conversations about what they might face, know who your audience is and what appeals to them, and be sure to practice, practice, practice.
- Make time to process your presentation. Highlight what worked well and make plans for next steps.

Up Next: Youth-Adult Partnerships

This chapter was a bit of a downer. We don't like talking about adults who are jerks. Chapter 15 shares fruitful examples of youth and district- or community-based adults working together to make change.

FIGURE 14.1 **Speaking truth to power**

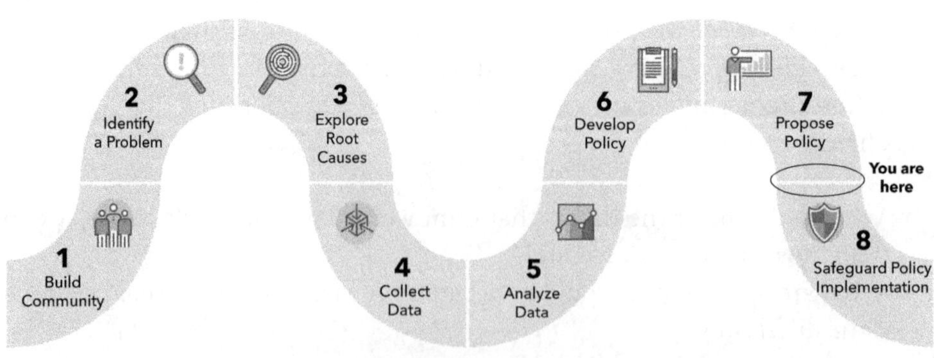

SECTION FIVE

Sustaining Your Work

TRANSFORMATIVE STUDENT VOICE DOES NOT end after the presentation; instead, it shifts into a new gear in which students work in partnership with adults to design and implement new policies and programs. In this section, we offer strategies and lessons for sustaining student voice work over several years, including ways to work in partnership, hold decision-makers accountable, and balance continuity and change as veteran students graduate and new students join projects. The book concludes with our vision for Transformative Student Voice in schools and districts.

FIFTEEN

Youth-Adult Partnerships

PRINCESS, A HIGH SCHOOL SOPHOMORE, stood on a stage with her peers and gazed out over a packed conference room. District officials, school board members, academics, community activists, and hundreds of peers stared back at her.

"Can anybody here name the three types of consent? Raise your hand if so." No hands were raised in the silent room. "See, no hands," Princess continued. "Why don't we have these conversations at our schools? We deserve the basic information regarding things like consent and our bodies. That's why . . . we have fought hard to make sure the comprehensive health curriculum gets taught this year."

Princess's introduction launched her and her classmates into a presentation about how they identified a problem around sexual consent in their school. Their investigation propelled them into a yearlong project working with district officials and some of the authors of this book to create and ensure the implementation of a comprehensive health course not only in their school but across the district.

It's not exactly what the young people set out to do, as sophomore Harrison explained during their presentation. "Our goal has varied throughout the year. At the start it was to create a sex ed class. Then it turned into an overall health class. It then changed to working alongside the curriculum creator to implement this class properly into our schools."

At this phase in the CCI process, after students have presented a policy solution to their research problem, a need for a new type of partnership with adult stakeholders tends to emerge between youth and the school or district officials who hold the power for change. In the case of Princess and her classmates, the students completed a terrific TSV project with their teacher about the need for a comprehensive health class and what content it would need to cover to meet the needs of the youth. To make that a lasting change in the district, however, they needed to work in collaboration with adults who were new to them, including, in this case, a curriculum coordinator, the student voice program coordinator, and academic partners from the local university.

While the potential for change is exciting, these types of relationships create a variety of new challenges and considerations. This chapter focuses on how to prepare students—and adults—to participate effectively in these kinds of new youth-adult partnerships, and it provides guidelines for how teams of young people and adults can work together, share power, and honor each other's experience and values in the name of impacting change. Just to be clear: this chapter is *not* about working with teachers or coaches, which we covered earlier in chapter 2. This is about the new and complicated concerns involving connections with school, district, or even community power players.

INVITING, RESEARCHING, ROLE-PLAYING

The students pushing for the health curriculum were driven by a social justice mission that they had developed after interviewing their peers about their knowledge of sexual health and consent. Their goal: students should enter adulthood with proper knowledge of their bodies and a clearer understanding of sexual consent.

The youth identified two major hurdles preventing them from acquiring this necessary knowledge: the beliefs of their parents and the social stigmas and taboos surrounding sex. During a presentation, an adult community member pushed them to justify those root causes. One student answered, "We saw it for ourselves and people around us in our lives" before expanding, specifically, about how religious beliefs often suppress these types of conversations. Another student shared, "Parents can be a big burden when it comes to expressing sexuality."

Clearly, finding ways for youth and adults to talk about health and sex was proving difficult.

They sharpened those skills and deepened their understanding of the issue when the youth set up a meeting with Carlos, a coauthor of this book. The youth, with the help of their teacher, sent Carlos an email with a clear time and place to meet. They also did some research on who he was and what his values were by searching his professional website and reading some of the articles he had written. It was clear that Carlos, whose research focused deeply on youth agency and action, could be an accomplice. The youth and their teacher also engaged in role-playing, with the teacher pretending to be Carlos and the students practicing how the meeting would flow. At the meeting, Carlos supported the students in thinking about research methods as part of the partnership between his university and the school district. During their presentation months later, the students said this meeting with Carlos allowed them to learn fundamental skills that supported their research. As one presenter said, "He helped us become more comfortable with the topic."

This is an excellent example of adults with expertise working with students on the young people's terms. Carlos gets props for coming prepared both in terms of his own self-awareness but also with clear, concise, and actionable ideas about how the students could leverage research to support their quest for a comprehensive health course. This exhibits some key considerations in holding youth-adult meetings. The youth, teacher, and Carlos all ensured that there was a youth-friendly meeting structure by having the youth set the time, space, and modality. While communication norms were not explicitly discussed, Carlos came to the space with "big ears and a small mouth." In other words, he was committed to listening before sharing his ideas. Teachers or coaches can play an important role in vetting partners; the teacher in this case already knew Carlos and how he would interact with the youth.

That may not always be the case. What if the adult says something condescending ("You guys are so cute")? What if the adult praises the policy but refuses to commit to change ("This is so cool that you're thinking about this, but I don't know if I can actually make anything change; I mean, with testing and the school calendar . . .")? If the adult visitor is more opposed to the youth work, or if the youth are unclear about the adult's values, the role-play or practice phase may need to be more intense and targeted. In our CCI curriculum, we share an activity where the teacher (or even another student) role-plays the president of a chamber of commerce blocking access to youth workforce opportunities. We advise students and teachers to run through the meeting three times. One is more friendly to the youth; one is almost comically against them; the third is somewhere in the middle. While the role-playing often gets silly, it does offer an opportunity to prepare youth for a variety of adult reactions.

STUDENTS AS SHOT-CALLERS

After the meeting with Carlos, the youth finalized an interview protocol. Their results were startling. Half of the high schoolers they talked to had never taken a sex ed course. More than 60 percent couldn't name the different types of consent. Some students didn't know what *STI* stood for or couldn't define *consent* in any way. The youth also interviewed their teachers. "A weird thing we found was that most of the teachers we interviewed *had* taken some sort of health course in high school," a student said during the presentation. "This led us to wonder, 'What happened?'"

That question led them to deepen relationships with two coordinators at the school district level. Estrella, the coordinator of the student voice and leadership program, planned an event where youth researchers could interact with district power players to better understand the problems they were investigating. As part of this event, the students who were focused on comprehensive health met Maria, a district curriculum coordinator in charge of health. The students and their teacher again prepared by researching both Estrella and Maria, practicing meetings, and anticipating a variety of reactions. In listening to the students, Maria quickly found that their interests converged; Maria was in the process of piloting a class similar to what the students were demanding at four larger high schools. Maria asked the students to review the curriculum, and they agreed, training their gaze on four main areas: age-appropriate activities, culturally responsive lessons and activities, lessons with importance, and time to understand each concept.

The students deeply examined the curriculum, which covered topics from nutrition to decision-making, and they worked with Maria to revise the lessons to make them more engaging. This included deepening a focus on mental health and adding more of a teen-focused lens around the various forms of consent. At the presentation, the students proudly shared, "Not only do we have a health teacher hired for next year, but we have three sections on our school's master schedule with a growing interest as we advertise the class." The audience applauded, with no one louder than Maria, who whooped and hollered from the back of the room before congratulating the students when they left the stage.

While the students and their teacher may not have explicitly intended to form long-term relationships with district officials, the partnerships proved beneficial. Estrella served as a sort of organization broker, revealing to the youth the complicated inner workings of the district. In essence, she helped them find the right person who could make the changes they wanted to see. That clarity allowed the youth to not get bogged down in the big, confusing district structure but to instead strike with precision by finding the right person quickly. In essence, she helped the youth navigate adult politics and, ultimately, helped them to achieve their desired impact. Too often youth are kept out of adult spaces and are limited by a lack of understanding of district or school bureaucracy.

Serendipitously, Maria was already open to working with youth. She listened, found common ground, and invited the students in as sort of curricular consultants. She could instead have been leery and stonewalled them. But most of all, Maria exhibited some best practices in this work (for more, see figure 15.1): she listened to student feedback and took action to meet their demands for the curriculum. Had she not, Estrella and the students would have followed up, ensuring accountability. But we're impressed with how Maria didn't hold an adultist, rigid line. We often get feedback from adults that student input in curriculum is inappropriate, or that students don't have the expertise to have an opinion. Maria did *not* adopt that stance, instead inviting youth feedback and actually responding to it. Certainly, her interest converged with the students in this case (they *all* wanted a strong health curriculum taught across the district), making for a natural and smooth relationship.

Their relationship didn't stop there. Estrella, the program coordinator, helped the students and Maria keep in touch. The students eventually requested to add a four-week Critical Civic Inquiry unit to the end of the health curriculum, where youth could have time to investigate one of the various health inequities they had discovered during the course of the health class.

FIGURE 15.1 **Do's and don'ts for adults in youth-adult partnerships**

Do...	Don't...
Listen for understanding when talking to students about their experiences.	Step in with assumptions that you know what youth want or don't want.
Understand that young people are like adults—we also want to learn and grow.	Talk more than the youth partners.
Be vulnerable.	Be condescending or talk down to students.
Be ready and willing to learn from young people.	Say, "That's not possible."
See youth as experts in the conversation.	Take things personally.
Share power and resources with young people.	Use youth for your own aims.

Note: Draft created by transformative student voice team of youth and adults (2022).

Not everything went smoothly. Almost a year after the project, some of the students expressed disappointment that not all their ideas for the curriculum were adopted. The youth also wanted a regular and active role in framing the curriculum and training teachers how to use it. That hasn't happened, they've said.

While the health project had some notable successes, we have also seen instances of school officials using youth as pawns to serve their agenda. Sometimes adults will influence the direction of a student voice project, either through suggestive influence (for example, touting the need for a certain policy) or by directly instructing youth to delete or include specific messages in their policy proposals. In one case we saw an adult administrator resort to threats of discipline to silence the voices of youth who were critical of her administration. Often students are forced to compromise. In the health curriculum case, they could have considered their limits for compromise. Did they have any nonnegotiables for this meeting? What if the nonnegotiables are not possible for some reason? What might be the next best solution? What if, for example, the district had just purchased a new health curriculum, and they weren't willing to revisit the topic for a number of years; what then? Considering when to negotiate and when to hold a hard line is tricky in these cases and certainly implicates the adult to be a strong partner with youth.

ACCOUNTABILITY FROM ADULTS AND YOUTH

Another example we observed underscored the need for both youth and adults to be accountable in order for these relationships to flourish. Students at one high school surveyed their classmates about microaggressions. They then presented their results to school staff and district administrators, along with a request to revise the English and social studies curricula to more centrally integrate experiences of Black and Brown Americans. They also asked to be part of redesigning the character education units for their peers as well as creating professional development for teachers. Finally, they demanded inclusion on the school's equity council.

As with all youth voice work, it's illuminating to follow up on what actually happened in response to those student-generated demands. We are not sure the students were ever included in the curriculum work, but that might have been due to disruption during the COVID-19 pandemic. By the time school returned to normal, those students had graduated. They did meet with the teacher team to design character education units, which were implemented. Some strategies named earlier, such as connecting with adults who were willing to listen and take student feedback seriously, were the biggest levers—researching power players and role-playing not so much. The students did meet with the equity council to design and present professional development units. They were invited to send reps to the equity council; those reps came a few times, but their schedules eventually got in the way.

In two other districts, as part of a School Climate Transformation Grant, young people have been working with the climate team to develop sensory pathways, wellness rooms, and policies for gender-neutral bathrooms. The grant required districts to have both a climate team (adults) and a student voice team, and for those teams to collaborate in some ways. It didn't happen the way we imagined it would, but we learned a lot about inviting youth into meetings and ensuring they'll keep coming.

When youth are invited into formal adult spaces, it is helpful for them to understand the norms of the group. How do they structure agendas? Do they operate by Robert's Rules of Order? Do they make decisions using consensus-based decision-making, or do they report to a leader who decides? Youth are then faced with a choice to accept, try to modify, or reject those norms. Returning to the equity council example earlier, the youth were invited to attend, but meetings took place immediately following the school day on Wednesdays. The young people almost never showed up because they had competing commitments. Even outside of class, the students were busy: *I wanted to come but I needed to get help with homework; Mom needed me; my friends were chilling.* Instead of being judgmental or punitive, we urge adults to proactively anticipate these difficulties and to schedule and structure meetings with extreme empathy for the young person's head and heart. As we've said before, youth agency should outweigh adult comfort. But, to the youth, *Show up!* We know life is hard, but don't prove them right. If you truly can't make a meeting or appointment, you have choices: communicate, send a proxy, try to reschedule. Part of being taken seriously is being serious about the problem you're researching and the work it will take to solve it. Transformative Student Voice is not only about the permission to say "This sucks," but is also an obligation for youth to be active players in its solution.

Adults can't fix something they don't know is broken, so young people advocating for themselves is paramount. Youth should be prepared with responses to what might come up regarding things like meeting structure and the context and setting of the gathering. Consider worst-case scenarios: What happens if you get stumped or lost? What happens if the adult is a jerk? On the other end, what happens if they meet all your demands and more?

ORGANIZATIONAL STRUCTURES

In many cases, like the high schoolers and their curricular demands, these projects live in isolation, onetime efforts that are gone with the graduating class. The new group often chooses a new issue, leaving the previous work behind. While that makes sense given the traditional schooling calendar, it's not ideal for lasting school reform. Some of the biggest youth voice gains we have seen take multiple years to accomplish. One team worked on their youth voice project for four years before achieving a victory. The key to long-term impact lies in examining organizational structures and identifying a designated point person who ensures that students are included on design, planning, and hiring teams. This may look different depending on the district. In our health example from earlier, the students attended a massive district and needed to connect with more niche power players to make change. Estrella, from the student voice and leadership program, and Maria, the health curriculum lead, proved to be those people. Finding that right, nuanced connection proved a fruitful, long-term partnership.

Your team could start by examining the organizational structure of the district: who is in charge of what? Then, use your research skills to uncover more about what motivates each of those people. Are they responsible for student safety? For achievement? What are the teams or committees that are working on various issues? (Your school board agendas or notes might help with this.) Once you know who is doing what—and why—consider where you need to be to move your work forward. Should you ask to be included in the working group that is revising the code of conduct? Is the curriculum team the place to be?

Once youth know where they want to be, they may need help getting strategic in figuring out how to be invited in and how to engage once they get there. This includes learning about the norms for each of the groups. It also requires making a commitment to showing up and coming prepared. It means being aware of when youth are being heard and when youth are being used. It requires practicing how youth are going to speak up and call out problematic behavior. It implicates youth in planning to offer solutions to the problems they identify.

In smaller districts, we've seen superintendents leverage youth councils to empower students to have a say in school vision and operations. While these can be empowering for young people, we've also seen those councils tokenize and co-opt youth work. While students and educators can work together to prepare for and nurture relationships with district personnel and administrators, much of the onus is on the adult to leave their potentially adultist ways behind and genuinely engage with youth with their best interests at heart. A large part of that is adults knowing their identities and epistemology. They must engage in critical self-reflection to root out assumptions and biases about themselves and students. Is there any place in the school, for example, where student voice should *not* be? (We take this question up explicitly in our companion book, *Transformative Student Voice: Partnering with Young People for Equitable School Improvement.*[1]) Should they have a say in teacher and administrator evaluation? Should they be part of the hiring committees? Should they help design the curriculum? It's important to know where your line is. We know there are some things that youth aren't prepared to do safely by themselves—a three-year-old crossing a busy street alone, for example, is dangerous. When it comes to older students critiquing school systems, think about where your line is and why it might exist in that spot. Often adults are afraid—afraid that the young people will fail; afraid of breaching ethics, or of school or public reaction; afraid that it will all be a waste of time, and the youth won't learn. As we hope this book is revealing, youth research can have a deep impact both for the student and the community.

Often that work involves sustaining a project over several years as school populations shift (as we saw with COVID-19 impacting the high schoolers' curriculum demands). We explore those challenges in the next chapter.

QUESTIONS FOR ADULTS AS THEY PREPARE TO PARTNER WITH YOUNG PEOPLE

- Think about your meeting structure: is it youth-friendly?
- What are the norms for communicating in meetings? How will you co-construct those to allow for fuller youth participation?
- How will agendas be constructed? Do youth get to create, add, give feedback?
- How will decisions be made? Consensus? Vote? Leaders take input then choose?
- How will conflict be named and mediated?
- Will you use grouping strategies to ensure all voices are heard before sharing with the larger group? What about processing time? How will you attend to power and patterns of participation?
- What is the size of the group? How does that impact the process? Are students the smallest group? How to allow for that not to feel tokenistic?
- What accountability do adults have for engaging and communicating with students?

CONCLUSION

Key Takeaways

- Students practicing or preparing for interactions with adults can help smooth the process.

- Adults should also prepare, including thinking about when and where the meeting will take place and how adults can support youth in the space.
- Accountability goes both ways. Youth need to show up at the meetings and participate. Adults need to work to enact youth change.
- Understanding organizational structures is key to understanding one another and the possible change that can occur.

Up Next: Balancing Continuity and Change

With so much cool work and thinking done, it's time to think a bit about how to keep your projects churning despite inevitable change like the end of the school year and graduating team members.

FIGURE 15.2 **Partnering for change**

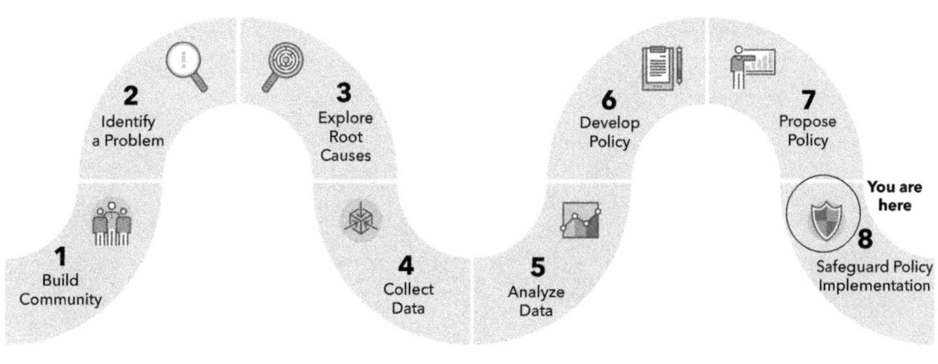

SIXTEEN

Balancing Continuity and Change

THE FINAL EXAM IN ONE TSV class we observed didn't look or feel like any test we had previously seen. The teacher asked each student to prepare and deliver a presentation that analyzed the team's strength, isolated an area for improvement, and shared a legacy item that next year's class could leverage for success.[1]

The first student to present lamented how seniors, including himself, seemed to lose focus and motivation at the end of the year. That, he said, caused the entire classroom community to suffer. As a response, his legacy item included a variety of icebreaker games that could be done in person or online to perhaps keep next year's class more tightly connected. Another student left not an item but a reminder about mindset. "Just share how you are feeling. If you are someone who is listening, be respectful, be open, don't judge them. The key to winning is being vulnerable." Another student's legacy item included an icebreaker routine she had learned at church. She translated that learning into a process that she and her classmates could use the following year, involving the teacher giving instructions and the students setting an agenda and then splitting up to accomplish various tasks before returning and debriefing the new learning.

While this example is about an assessment—developing authentic assessments for Transformative Student Voice is a current research focus—this chapter is about more than that. We are impressed with how the teacher and students were looking both backward *and* forward at the end of the process, critiquing their impact but also formulating steps for the future. This ensures that students care about the project and community while still having some choice and agency in the way the classroom functions and how learning occurs. This will, hopefully, sustain the young people's interest and efforts from one school year to the next. This is especially important—but counterintuitive, given the way schools have traditionally operated. A school year is nine months long with a three-month gap in between. Each year is siloed from ones that come before and after. Classes last one semester or one year. The thought of taking a class again is not just absurd; in many cases it is a sign of failure (you didn't pass it the first time).

The transformative student actions we support may not be attainable in one nine-month school year—in fact, we know of teams that have taken four school years to achieve their policy goals. In other words, meaningful change can take time, and this often doesn't jibe with school calendars. TSV projects can and often do take place over several years and with multiple cohorts of students. How is it possible to keep these projects churning with a new group of students and educators? How do they hold decision-makers accountable? Our aim in this chapter is to explore these questions further and provide some tangible insights on creating continuity.

SCHOOL-BASED EXAMPLES OF CONTINUITY AMID CHANGE

We will share the stories of educators and students who were able to maintain momentum over years and the specific strategies that supported them. One middle and high school advocated for student-led professional development for teachers five years ago; they've been leading it ever since, refining curriculum and fostering teacher-student relations. Another group of youth spent more than five years researching and requesting approaches to admit a more racially and socioeconomically diverse student body. And the teacher from the opening of this chapter established what she called a *cascade of leadership*, with seniors mentoring juniors while younger students received more direct support from the educator and student leaders. It is worth noting that these examples come from multiage clubs or classes within the school where students could participate for multiple years. We acknowledge that this may not be feasible in some classrooms or schools. Still, in each case, the educators and students worked to not only address the social justice issue they were researching but to ensure that a team of rising students were ready to continue the work.

Student-Led Professional Development

Students at Urban Arts Magnet (UAM) noticed a problem at their school: teachers and students didn't have good relationships and, at times, were adversarial toward each other. The students identified cultural barriers and prejudices as the root cause of the issue, and they proposed designing and leading a professional development unit (PDU) for their teachers on culturally responsive teaching—grounded in the cultural realities of students at the school. They proposed the plan for the PDU at the end of the 2018–19 school year; several of the students who proposed the plan graduated that year. During the next year, 2019–20, this group (including some continuing students from the previous year and some new students) worked with their teacher and district personnel to plan and develop the PDU units. Despite some questions and requested revisions, district officials were mostly on board with the idea of student-led professional development and helped the young people gain approval. The next academic year, 2020–21, the students at UAM implemented the PDU, with teachers earning professional district credit for the sessions. The young people then engaged in deep reflection and revision of the PDU and offered it again the following year. They have continued to offer the PDU up to the time of this book's printing.

The PDU is now not only a mainstay at UAM, but the students have supported other TSV teams in designing their own professional development sessions. One school is offering a PDU on sharing power with students through curriculum. Another is running adult and student professional development through morning advisory blocks. The district, too, has featured UAM's PDU model as an exemplar, and they encourage other schools to emulate it. We are impressed by several parts of this story. First, the students devised the idea and content for youth-led professional development in response to a problem they observed. Second, district officials actually approved the project and later helped amplify its message and impact. Finally, and most of all, we are impressed at how generations of students have picked up the PDU spirit and process and kept it not only alive but flourishing. This is a testament to how one team was able to promote continuity of their project over multiple years.

Socioeconomic Diversity Project

Students at another arts school in the same district, Creative Arts Academy (CAA), had years ago identified a lack of diversity as a problem at the school (we touched on this story in chapter 9). Diversifying a school, while noble and important, doesn't happen quickly. Students at CAA researched this problem for at least five years. In that time several of the researchers have graduated, but their younger classmates kept picking it up with the help of their teacher, who continued to lead the student research group from year to year. While the theme of diversifying the student body remains, the group's focus and impact shift slightly each year as they deepen their research. Initially, the students explored how the school's rigid conservatory model and audition process excluded students of color and those living in poverty. In following years, the students implemented and researched a mentorship program aimed at fostering an interest in the arts among younger students in order to hopefully diversify CAA in the future.

More recently, the students have explored "social issues that enforce exclusivity and elitism" at CAA. The youth have worked with the administration to reenvision teacher hiring and student recruitment practices. The school is in the midst of expanding their campus facilities, and the student researchers are working with administrators as closely as possible to use this growth as an opportunity to diversify the school. We find the CAA students' dedication and foresight impressive. They have stuck with an important but difficult issue. The group has tried different approaches to advance their cause, including building a coalition with the administration, and within the group they have instilled a value and appreciation for diversity that sustains the group's work year over year.

Cascade of Leadership

In one program we support, students can take the same class for multiple years in high school, earning an array of credits (mostly elective) for their student voice and leadership work. Joni, the teacher from the intro of this chapter, has taught that class. The final exam described in the introduction is where Joni started when thinking about leadership continuity. At the start of a new school year, both the reflections and legacy items could be leveraged with returning and new students.

Another key component to continuity is how Joni differentiates student roles. In a new school year, returning students begin the process of examining the reflections of graduating team members and assessing the strengths and limitations of the previous year's work. Meanwhile, Joni pulls the newer members into a group and works with them through more baseline understandings needed in the course, such as a short reading on the twelve types of oppression. In this sort of differentiated classroom, older students can flash their expertise and leadership while younger students build those skills.

If you've ever spent time in high school classrooms, you know that about halfway through the year, seniors start checking out. No shade to them—it's natural to focus on the next step of life as one chapter closes. But that did something beautiful in Joni's class: it created a power vacuum that younger students could fill. In our observations, we saw one sophomore spend the entire first quarter silent, but in the second semester, they volunteered to kick off the class's presentation in front of the principal and school board members. We saw another student initially show confusion around the class's research project but months later created an artistic representation of the problem that powerfully reframed the issue for classmates. The next year, both of those students became upper-level leaders of the team.

Through a forward-looking final, differentiated approaches with new and returning students, and supporting younger students in filling the void left by senior leaders, Joni was able to establish some form of continuity from year to year.

TAKEAWAYS

We notice some common themes across these examples. First, the students in all of these teams are awesome. They identified creative, student-centered solutions to real problems facing them and their schools. Recruiting students who fit this work is a major consideration. If you teach TSV as a class, it may be an elective. How can you frame it to appeal to students who would be interested in and benefit from taking civic action in schools and communities? Along the way, consider students who might not fit the traditional profile of being a leader, but who might have unique lived insights into the problem your team seeks to address. We will say more about this in a bit.

If you run TSV more as a club, you may have more freedom in who you recruit. What kinds of student values, traits, and dispositions are the right fit? Though we've often found that typical leaders (with high GPAs and many extracurricular achievements on their resume) can flourish within a TSV approach, we're more interested in appealing to students who exhibit a fire for justice and activism—those who make interesting connections in classroom discussions, those who may resist certain policies or rules, those who ask compelling questions and push teachers for more explanation. When these students engage in TSV, they really come to life. Suddenly they are engaged and interested in school, and they have a lived experience that can push the thinking of your TSV team. Remember, for student voice to flourish, we need the perspectives of *all* youth!

Second, the educator in each example stayed the same. As students graduated and new classroom communities formed, the teacher remained consistent. While TSV is a student-led approach, adults are important partners. They can help pass on and translate experience and knowledge between students and student groups. Good TSV educators also broker deep and meaningful relationships with administration and other power players. The longer they stay, often, the deeper those relationships go, and the more mutual respect is built.

Finally, the solutions were worth enacting and supporting. Each of these examples did not include tokenized actions or onetime events. In other words, the solution is worth fighting for. And when that is the case, it typically takes more than one school year. It is relatively easy to plan a project whose culmination is a onetime event, such as a teach-in or a presentation. But to actually change policies that disrupt business as usual takes time and alliances, as we discuss further in chapter 17.

These three points are not an exhaustive list of what it takes to balance continuity and change when doing TSV work. In fact, it's probably woefully incomplete. And maybe that's a good thing. What worked for Joni, in other words, may not work for every teacher in their own context. Educators need to find what works for them in their classroom community.

CHALLENGES, BENEFITS, AND DILEMMAS

We want to be super clear about how hard this work is, especially in classrooms with eclectic identities, but also how beneficial it can be. We will spend some time in this section discussing the challenges of maintaining continuity—but also exploring the benefits.

Challenges

What fires up one cohort of students may not be the same for the next cohort. There often comes a tricky moment when a project is either picked up by the next group of youth or is rejected for something new. While difficult, it's important for everyone to not see this as a defeat or disrespect toward past researchers. In fact, there might be a sense of urgency with the new project that even past team members pick up on. Additionally, we've seen students return to TSV research from many years prior to help inform a new project.

If your class is completely turning over, how do you hand off the project to the next class? Joni had some ideas about that, starting with the final, which reflected on one year while setting a solid foundation for the next. The legacy items that Joni collected as part of the final were tangible best practices that could launch the next cohort's work.

A major consideration, then, is that students in the next cohort have a choice about whether to continue the project. We suggest launching the year with a gallery walk of sorts that includes examples from the previous year, including the focal problem, root cause analysis, counternarrative, research findings, policy documents, and more. This allows the new students to understand what's been done before, see how they connect to it, and determine whether they are excited about it moving forward. The consensus process we've mentioned throughout the book is good to leverage after the gallery walk. Can everyone live with this problem as the focus for our work? If the answer is no, then you start the process (and book) over again, building community, selecting a new problem, and so on. While that may seem daunting, it could also be refreshing as the educator to support students in exploring something new.

Benefits

Sticking with one problem across years and cohorts can be deeply rewarding. We saw that in the examples earlier in this chapter, where students worked to deliver youth-led professional development, diversify their school, and craft a cascade of leadership. Students often get fired up to be working on something real, not just a school assignment. This excitement alone could be worth fostering and supporting over time. And, perhaps, we have a moral obligation to keep the doors of action research and activism open to students. In other words, exposing youth to things like YPAR and TSV often changes the way they see themselves and the world around them, while also giving them a framework to take action and make change. In fact, our research has shown that when youth have multiple years of TSV engagement, the young people are more likely to be engaged in social action in their schools and communities.[2] This fact fires us up as a team: engaging in TSV over multiple years prepares students to be civically engaged citizens in the present.

As educators, we know that school and society are often in tension. While we want students to make real change with issues impacting their lives, it will usually take more than one school year of the TSV experience. Sustaining projects across years and cohorts is more authentic to real-world organizing and civic engagement. In civic life, victories may take years to be achieved—and losses are usually sustained along the way. Therefore, trying something out, learning from it, and trying again are key skills. Additionally, most organizing groups encounter changes in membership, with new members joining the cause along the way. Thus, learning how to onboard new members and sustain momentum of a project is key. So yes, it sucks, and it can be hard to impact change in one year, but learning about sustaining a multiyear project can be helpful in the long run.

Dilemmas

One of the key dilemmas as you balance continuity and change in your context is how, as the adult, to avoid becoming the face and name of the project. We noted earlier that our examples were successful because the teacher remained consistent. The risk is that they might seize control of the project, making it their personal charge. Joni mediated this by supporting the cascade of leadership: each year two or more students were rising to become leaders and set the research agenda. Those leaders, with Joni's support, were the ones to decide whether to pick up the previous year's work or to reject it and try something new. While that may not work for you, finding a way to support and not dominate the youth work is key. And that may include letting the young people decide to walk away from a project that you as an adult have been working on for years. As Dane often says, youth agency should outweigh teacher comfort.

CONCLUSION

Key Takeaways

- Real change can take time; having a plan in place to develop continuity from one year to the next is key.
- Though it sucks that you might not get a policy win within one school year's time, recognize that most social movements take time to achieve their goal. In taking on a project over multiple years, you might help young people learn skills they can take with them into civic life.
- It is also okay to move on from a legacy project. Maybe the youth are driven by something that is new and more urgent. As an adult, don't let your agenda get in the way of their agency.

TIPS TO MAINTAIN CONTINUITY AMID CHANGE

- *Build student-centered structures.* The students and educator at UAM worked with district officials to create student-led professional-development units. By going through proper district channels, the youth have an official stage from which they can work to educate their teachers.
- *Continue the work in layers.* It may take years to peel back the layers of big problems. The CAA students leaned into that, examining different contributing factors to the lack of diversity at their school and taking different forms of action each year.
- *Broker connections.* While the youth have their own impressive agency, how can you as an adult help them connect and strengthen relationships with powerful adults? In other words, consider how you can be an accomplice, creating connections to help move students' policy ideas forward.
- *Start at the end.* Consider having a final exam or reflection that explicitly considers continuity and how to hand off the project or group to new members.
- *Offer different paths.* Learning to be an activist takes time. Students newer to these ideas may need more support. Students with expertise may need quicker lanes to leadership.
- *Fill the void.* Seniors check out. Students transfer schools. Other stuff happens that will break up the team or class. Be deliberate about who is leaving and offer support to those returning to step up.

  (For a variety of resources, visit TransformativeStudentVoice.net.)

WHAT TO AVOID AT THIS STAGE

- *Expecting fast change.* Big problems take time to solve.
- *Getting too attached to a project.* If the kids aren't into it, ditch it.
- *Winging it.* Sustained change needs a plan, in this case one that spans cohorts and years. Winging it isn't going to cut it.

Up Next: From Empowerment to Power

Now that you've thought about multiyear engagement, it's time to take your goals to the next level: TSV as a tool for youth claiming power.

FIGURE 16.1 **Balancing continuity and change**

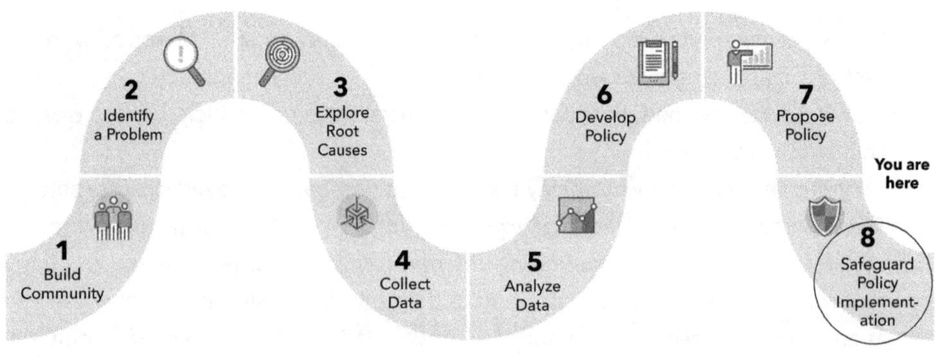

SEVENTEEN

From Empowerment to Power: Transformative Student Voice

CONGRATULATIONS! YOU HAVE REACHED the end of this book, and gained the tools and knowledge to facilitate TSV with your students. Our vision for this book is that it will accompany you on your journey as a youth voice facilitator or coach. Although some of you may be reading this in preparation for future TSV or YPAR projects, many of you have presumably led your students through some, if not all, elements of the action research cycle. Please know that facilitating TSV is unpredictable and full of challenges, even setbacks, but also highly rewarding. You will likely have to lead students through several cycles before you start to develop confidence in your skills as a facilitator. With more practice, you'll start to anticipate the challenges and missteps. You'll see where it makes sense to assert your expertise and where you can step back and leave room for students to claim their power.

In your first few experiences as a facilitator, you might focus on carrying out a strong project where students exercise their agency, collect and analyze data, and share their ideas with public audiences. This experience itself—especially communicating a policy call to action for decision-makers—can be exhilarating for students, even if you don't get the policy changes you are calling for. We live in a society where young people are rarely, if ever, invited into decision-making spaces. Gaining access to these spaces, and sharing their perspectives and policy arguments, is a *big win*. In our research, young people often talk about these encounters with public officials or decision-makers as the most exciting and challenging parts of their experience and therefore, where they experienced the most growth and learning. This has been true even when young people did not get the results they wanted. We have seen young people rejected by school principals, dismissed by school board members, and condescended to by state legislators. We have seen political figures take the credit for work led by youth and schoolteachers and refuse to listen to students who don't have a 3.0 GPA. In a social context where it is *so rare* for youth to speak up in civic and political spaces, just the experience of speaking your truth and offering a call to action is powerful and empowering. If you can get to this place with your team, it is a beautiful thing.

WHAT EMPOWERMENT LOOKS LIKE

> "Oh my god, I'm being listened to," she recounts. "I'm about to really bring it! . . . I'm not even going to shut up. I'm finally being listened to!"
>
> —youth leader in California

> I used to not be able to stand in front of ten people. If there was ten people's eyes on me, I would freeze and look away, or I wouldn't want to be there. I'd be like "Okay, I'm getting a phone call" or "Oh, I need to use the restroom" and disappear for the amount of time that I had to stand in front of people. That was one of the difficult things I've had to go through—speaking in front of a lot of people. But . . . I broke out . . . I broke out of that isolation of speech that I had.
>
> —youth leader in Colorado

But here's the thing. As you take pride in the speeches, and celebrate the thoughtful policy presentations, we don't want you to stop there. Yes, TSV has the potential to create profound feelings of empowerment among youth. But don't settle for empowerment. It's time to level up. TSV is not just about inculcating better self-esteem, confidence, or sense of agency in students; it is also about changing their external realities—the institutions and material conditions of their everyday lives. It calls for moving from empowerment to power.

What is the difference between empowerment and power, you might ask? Both are desirable, no doubt. Empowerment is a part of TSV and other youth voice work. Empowered youth are more confident in the public sphere; they don't just accept the world as it is but see it through a critical and imaginative lens. Empowered youth want more. They are willing to hold others accountable for following through on their promises and values. They feel *entitled*: as in, entitled to be treated with respect and to grow up in supportive communities and engaging schools. If the young people you work with are feeling more empowered after completing an action research cycle, that is a win.

But empowerment has its limits. It's a feeling. It's psychological, not political. It is self-belief, but not necessarily the ability to do something. What happens when the crew of students who feel empowered by participating in TSV move on? They may be transformed internally by the process, but the external conditions that the next classes will experience at your school haven't changed.

That's why, once you have some experience facilitating TSV, we are asking you to step up your game. We want you to start thinking about *power*, not just empowerment. Power, in contrast to empowerment, is a force that enables your students to compel others to change their decisions and behaviors. It goes beyond feeling powerful, to the ability to take steps to claim authority and transform one's reality. Treating student voice as a political project, and not just an educational exercise, is risky. It is far more threatening to decision-makers.

POWER

> Power, properly understood, is the ability to achieve purpose. It is the strength required to bring about social, political, or economic changes.[1]
>
> —Martin Luther King Jr.

> Power is "the potential to shape our lives and the world around us . . . [This] capacity isn't always exercised, or overt, but that doesn't mean it doesn't exist."[2]
>
> —Richard Healey and Sandra Hinson

We have witnessed countless scenes where decision-makers listen politely to students and applaud their words without responding to the substance of what students said. They celebrate the interaction as evidence of youth empowerment but do nothing to concede their power. Consider the example in the box below and reflect on the prompts that follow.

What Makes You Guys So Cool?

A group of middle schoolers have assembled behind the podium at their district's monthly school board meeting. Dressed in navy blue and khaki school uniforms, they are here to present their research and offer a call to action about improving facilities at their school. The students, with facilitation from their teacher, have spent five months engaged in the action research cycle, including photodocumentation comparing their school to a higher-resourced middle school just a few miles away. They share their desire to bring positive change for their school. They end their presentation calling for the school board to take action to improve their school facilities, and then ask, "Any questions?"

After a brief pause, one of the school board members raises their hand, leans into the mic, and says, "I have one question. What makes you guys *so* cool?" With this comment, the students are ushered away from the podium, the audience applauds, and the meeting proceeds to its next agenda item. Public comment is over.

- What did that question from the school board member accomplish?
- How would you have felt if you had been the students' teacher?
- What would have to happen for the school board to consider this proposal with more seriousness?

In our view, as successful as the student project was, and as flawless as their presentation was, the team lacked a political strategy. They thought that by making a moral argument, accompanied by evidence from their project, their policy proposals would be considered. This was naive. As much as we like to say schools are laboratories for democracy, they are not. Schools operate more on principles of feudalism than democracy. Formal lines of authority and obedience flow in one direction. Principals are hand selected and supervised by the district office. Teachers are accountable to their principals. Uptake of student ideas depends on the decision of the person in power rather than any democratic accountability.

Student presentations are treated as requests or recommendations rather than demands. Principals have very little incentive to partner with or concede to student demands. Students graduate; they move on. Principals can wait them out.

In this kind of organizational context, TSV teams that want to make an impact on material conditions in their schools need to have a strategy to elevate their power. They need to be able to go into their interactions with decision-makers not just dependent on the goodwill of their audiences. To do this, we briefly offer a way of thinking about power used by grassroots activists and organizers. It is called the *three faces of power*.

THE THREE FACES OF POWER

Why three faces? The creator of this framework, Steven Lukes, wanted to point us beyond the most visible expressions of power, or what he called the first face.[3] The first face, further explored in table 17.1, is what we imagine when we try to influence the decisions of others. TSV projects typically culminate with some version of the first face of power: they try to persuade a school leader or decision-maker to adopt a new policy, such as student participation on hiring teams or adding ethnic studies to the curriculum. The first face of power is integral to a change strategy, but it is often insufficient on its own.

TABLE 17.1 The three faces of power

DEFINITION	EXAMPLE
The first face: Trying to influence policymaking in visible decision-making arenas (such as school board meetings or school governance councils).	Students call for the school district to make it against regulations for police to handcuff students under the age of ten.
The second face: Building relationships with groups and organizations that are aligned around shared goals and will stand with each other in solidarity.	Students build a coalition in support of their agenda that includes parents, lawyers, and the teacher union; these allies contact the district and show up in support.
The third face: Using cultural beliefs, norms, traditions, and practices to shape the ways that people understand the world around them, their roles in the world, and what they see as possible.	Students use art (poetry, posters, drawings) to provoke adults to reflect on how strange it is that the district allows children to be handcuffed. Students create one-minute videos asking adults what happened to them when they broke school rules when they were children, to make the familiar strange.

The second face of power is, put simply, the power of coalitions. Students themselves, from one class or one club, have limited power to influence authority. But what if students are part of a broader coalition, like those we discussed in chapter 12? What if, instead of merely showing up as a group of four students to meet with the principal, there was also a network of parents who were there to show solidarity with the students? What if, when presenting a proposal to include students in teacher evaluation, the students had gotten the support of the teacher union?

The third face of power calls for even more patience and may take several years. Although one TSV team may not have the luxury of multiple years, there is still room for each team to chip away at this issue—see our suggestions for building continuity in chapter 16. In short, the third face of power is the arena of ideas, values, and worldview. It is the power to shape what is seen as normal and taken for granted as right and good. In this way it is perhaps the most influential type of power.

Consider, for example, an idea such as "student leadership." In conventional American schools, student leadership tends to be channeled into student councils that plan dances or spirit days. Woven into the common sense of US schools is the idea that students are the recipients of services; they are learners; they are incomplete and undeveloped. Even worse, they are seen as impulsive, emotional, and lacking the judgment that comes with a mature prefrontal cortex. In this context, it is of course logical that student leadership should be restricted to relatively innocuous activities like pajama days or yearbooks.

But what if your TSV team took on the common sense that students ought to be treated in this way? What if they offered an alternative conception of student leaders—as partners in decision-making with adults? To do this requires more than policy argument, and more than a coalition, but also an effort to disrupt the common sense of a school community. It might lead to TSV actions that include poetry, storytelling, or drama to illustrate the flaws of this common sense and get people to reconsider their assumptions about youth.

DON'T LET PERFECTION BE THE ENEMY OF THE GOOD

We invite you to see this work as long-term and developmental. Or, as Therese Quinn and Erica Meiners put it, "slow work."[4] You, as a teacher or facilitator, will get better over time. Set goals for yourself as you move forward in this work. The first time you do this, you might not even get to the policy presentation. Take satisfaction in the fact that you started to share power with students or that they had rich discussions about issues in their everyday lives and what they wanted to change. Maybe next time your team will send those emails to the principal with enough notice that she gets the meeting on her schedule before making budget decisions for the next year. Sure, she might decline your proposal, but your students have gotten a taste of voice and activism and want more. And, just as important, you've started to see how you can support your students in building the power they need to be taken seriously by decision-makers.

Just remember, each time you do it, try to level up. Don't be too hard on yourself; there will always be more mistakes than you can count. You will screw up something. You will wish you had handled a pivotal moment differently. But give yourself grace and encourage your students to do the same. Remember to pause regularly to reflect together. Celebrate achievements, even small ones. And then think about how to improve next time.

TOOLS FOR SELF-REFLECTION

For you as the facilitator:

- What is your greatest strength as a TSV facilitator? Where do you want to improve?
- Looking ahead to the next TSV cycle, whether one semester or one year, what are three skills you want to get better at? Skills include:
  - facilitating group decisions
  - training students in data analysis
  - helping students build coalitions
  - sharing power with students
- Looking ahead to the next three years, where do you want to be in this work? What networks do you want to be part of? How can you invite colleagues into this work?

For your students:

- What did we do well this year? What should we be proud of as a group?
- What did *you* do well this year? What is one thing that you learned or completed that *you* are proud of?

- How do you want to thank the team for how they showed up this year?
- What was the biggest challenge you encountered? How did you handle it? How might you handle it next time?
- What advice can you give to me for when I facilitate a project next year? What advice do you have for next year's students?

CONCLUSION

As you move forward in this work, you may get frustrated that you are having to always go it alone. This work is too important to be carried out in isolation. Find your allies. Join networks.

NO MORE LONE WOLVES

Dane Stickney

After a terrible first year teaching a canned curriculum in oppressive ways, I wanted to change my practice. Critical Civic Inquiry and Transformative Student Voice provided me the will and ways to remake the sixth-grade writing class I taught into a more humanizing, inviting, and critical space. It took hard work and planning, but the approach landed deeply with students. They quickly enjoyed forming a circle and engaging in conversations about identity and social inequities that we could explore as a class. I beamed at the freedom they showed, tossing out ideas and adding onto each other while not raising their hands or sitting in proper posture.

My principal, however, hated it. After seeing the students explore the power that comes with citizenship and documentation in an organic and impassioned way, my principal did not share my excitement and pride. Instead, she put me on an improvement plan because I was breaking school norms about how and where students sat and how and when students participated in discussion. From that point forward, she mandated, all students would have to be in their seats with proper posture and sharing only after raising their hands.

I played the game. The students and I kept most of our practices, but we were sneaky. We often had two objectives and a second, *academic* packet of material at the ready in case we were observed. Ultimately, those tactics weren't necessary.

Soon after the improvement plan was levied, our school got formative standardized test scores back. I was teaching four classes. In two classes where I did *not* use the TSV approach, students scored well, racking up an average of one year's growth in half a year's time. In the classes where I taught TSV, the data was ridiculous. One class grew 2.4 years in half a year's time; the other grew 2.8 years. Upon seeing the data, by far the highest in our network of schools, the principal tore up the improvement plan and told me to keep on doing what I had been doing. I was barely observed by her the rest of the year, but TSV researchers and academics regularly rolled through, giving me the feedback and support I craved.

I formed a community with other teachers pursuing their master's degrees, and we worked together to support each other through the difficult work of doing TSV in classrooms. Now, as a teacher educator, I still seek out those kinds of teachers, ones fed up with status quo approaches and looking to do more powerful and meaningful work. The Curriculum and Instruction master's program at the University of Colorado Denver is a wonderful place to push such practice in a community that shares those values. The Action Research Network of the Americas is a soft and welcoming organization seeking to support practitioners of action research, including YPAR. Many state and national organizations support these progressive teaching approaches, as well. But at its heart, this can be lonely, isolating, and challenging work. It takes bravery and toughness. We at TSV get it. We are here to help however we can.

If you are interested in learning more about how to create systems and structures for Transformative Student Voice at the district level, check out our companion volume, *Transformative Student Voice: Partnering with Young People for Equitable School Improvement.*[5] Better yet, buy it for your principal and invite them to join your reading group. We also invite you to reach out to us, the authors of this book, to keep the work moving forward: www.TransformativeStudentVoice.net.

Key Takeaways

- TSV leads to feelings of empowerment, but don't stop there.
- Change in institutions and systems requires your students to claim their power.
- Students claim power not just by speaking up in decision-making settings, but also by building alliances and disrupting people's notions about what is possible.

Up Next

Congratulations! You're done! (At least for now; we're guessing you have a long list of actions you'd like to take.)

FIGURE 17.1 **Transforming education systems**

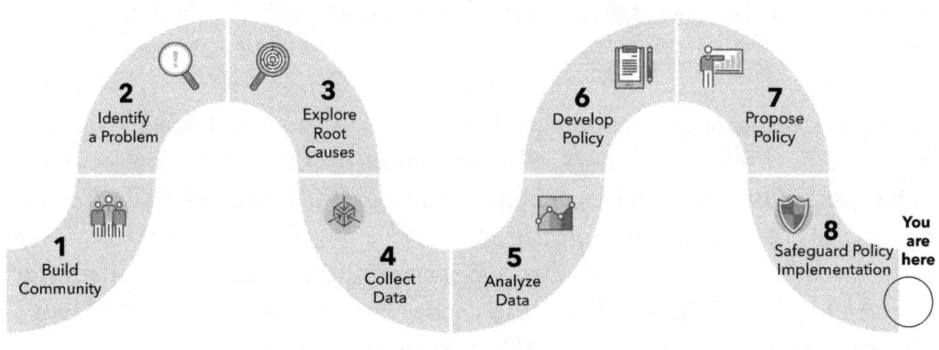

Notes

Section 1

1. Shelley Zion, Ben Kirshner, and Carlos P. Hipolito-Delgado, *Transformative Student Voice: Partnering with Young People for Equitable School Improvement* (Cambridge, MA: Harvard Education Press, forthcoming 2025).

Chapter 1

1. Allan G. Johnson, *Privilege, Power, and Difference,* 2nd ed. (New York: McGraw-Hill, 2005).
2. "Characteristics of Public School Teachers," from *The Condition of Education 2023* (Washington, DC: National Center for Education Statistics, 2023), https://nces.ed.gov/programs/coe/pdf/2023/clr_508.pdf.
3. John Bell, *Understanding Adultism: A Major Obstacle to Developing Positive Youth-Adult Relationships* (Somerville, MA: YouthBuild USA, March 1995), https://actioncivics.scoe.net/pdf/Understanding_Adultism.pdf.
4. Bell, *Understanding Adultism*.
5. Bell, *Understanding Adultism*, 5.
6. Shelley Zion, Adam York, and Dane Stickney, "Bound Together: White Teachers/Latinx Students Revising Resistance," *The Power of Resistance: Culture, Ideology and Social Reproduction in Global Contexts,* ed. Rowhea M. Elmesky, Carol Camp Yeakey, and Olivia Marcucci (Bingley, UK: Emerald Publishing, 2017), 429–58, https://doi.org/10.1108/S1479-358X20140000012020.
7. Zion, York, and Stickney, "Bound Together."
8. Dane Stickney, Elizabeth Milligan Cordova, and Carlos P. Hipolito-Delgado, "Get Out of Your Own Way: Sharing Power to Engage Students of Color in Authentic Conversations of Social Inequity," in *Making Classroom Discussions Work: Methods for Quality Dialogue in the Social Studies*, ed. Jane C. Lo (New York: Teachers College Press, 2022), 176–91.

Chapter 2

1. Sepehr Vakil and Maxine M. de Royston, "Exploring Politicized Trust in a Racially Diverse Computer Science Classroom," *Race Ethnicity and Education* 22, no. 4 (April 2019): 545–67, https://doi.org/10.1080/13613324.2019.1592846.

2. Throughout the book, we use pseudonyms to refer to all people and places other than our research team, so as to protect the anonymity of participants in research per the requirements of our IRB. This pseudonym is pronounced "nah-dare," meaning "rare" in Farsi.
3. Madeline Fox and Michelle Fine, "Accountable to Whom? A Critical Science Counter-Story About a City That Stopped Caring for Its Young," *Children and Society* 27, no. 4 (July 2013): 321–35, https://doi.org/10.1111/chso.12031.
4. Luis Valdez, *Pensamiento Serpentino* (Houston, TX: Arte Publico Press, 1973).
5. "Youth Engaged in Leadership and Learning," John W. Gardner Center for Youth and Their Communities, https://gardnercenter.stanford.edu/projects/youth-engaged-leadership-and-learning.

Chapter 3

1. Shelley Zion, Adam York, and Dane Stickney, "Bound Together: White Teachers/Latinx Students Revising Resistance," *The Power of Resistance: Culture, Ideology and Social Reproduction in Global Contexts,* ed. Rowhea M. Elmesky, Carol Camp Yeakey, and Olivia Marcucci (Bingley, UK: Emerald Publishing, 2017), 429–58, https://doi.org/10.1108/S1479-358X20140000012020.
2. Guardian News, "Emma Gonzalez's Powerful March for Our Lives Speech in Full," March 24, 2018, 7:03, https://www.youtube.com/watch?v=u46HzTGVQhg.
3. Guardian News, "Greta Thunberg to World Leaders: 'How Dare You? You Have Stolen My Dreams and My Childhood," September 23, 2019, 4:34, https://www.youtube.com/watch?v=TMrtLsQbaok.
4. Christopher Paul Curtis, *Bud, Not Buddy* (New York: Delacorte Press, 1999).

Chapter 4

1. Paulo Freire, *Pedagogy of the Oppressed* (New York: Continuum, 1970).
2. Julio Cammarota and Michelle Fine, *Revolutionizing Education: Youth Participatory Action Research in Motion* (New York: Routledge, 2008), 226.
3. RHS PBL Team, "Kid President How to Disagree," April 2, 2017, 4:18, https://www.youtube.com/watch?v=dG5fkAgJmqc.
4. Ursula K. Le Guin, "The Ones Who Walk Away from Omelas," in *The Wind's Twelve Quarters: Short Stories* (New York: Harper & Row, 1975), 275–84.
5. The Opportunity Atlas, https://www.opportunityatlas.org/.
6. Aatish Bhatia and Claire Cain Miller, "Explore How Income Influences Attendance at 139 Top Colleges," *New York Times*, September 11, 2023, https://www.nytimes.com/interactive/2023/09/11/upshot/college-income-lookup.html; Lena V. Groeger, Annie Waldman, and David Eads, "Miseducation: Is There Racial Inequality at Your School," *Pro Publica*, October 16, 2018, https://projects.propublica.org/miseducation/; https://edtrust.org/.
7. Maritza Montero, "Methods for Liberation: Critical Consciousness in Action," in *Psychology of Liberation: Theory and Applications*, ed. Maritza Montero and Christopher C. Sonn (New York: Springer, 2009): 73–91.

8. Antwi A. Akom, Julio Cammarota, and Shawn Ginwright, "Youthtopias: Towards a New Paradigm of Critical Youth Studies," *Youth Media Reporter* 2, no. 4 (August 2008): 1–30.
9. Roderick J. Watts, Jaleel K. Abdul-Adil, and Terrance Pratt, "Enhancing Critical Consciousness in Young African American Men: A Psychoeducational Approach," *Psychology of Men and Masculinity* 3, no. 1 (January 2002): 47, https://doi.org/10.1037/1524-9220.3.1.41.

Chapter 6

1. Aaron Schutz and Marie G. Sandy, *Collective Action for Social Change: An Introduction to Community Organizing* (New York: Palgrave Macmillan, 2011).
2. María Isabel Cortés-Zamora, Elizabeth Churape-García, and Nora Nuñez-Gonzalez, "Building Intellectual Warriors: Engaging Students in a Culturally Relevant Learning Environment," in *Educating for Social Justice: Field Notes from Rural Communities*, ed. Rebekah A. Cordova and William M. Reynolds (Leiden, Netherlands: Brill Sense, 2020), 107–39.
3. Abraham H. Maslow, "A Theory of Human Motivation," *Psychological Review* 50, no. 4 (July 1943): 370–96, https://doi.org/10.1037/h0054346.

Chapter 7

1. "California Educational Opportunity Report," UCLA Institute for Democracy, Education, and Access, https://idea.gseis.ucla.edu/educational-opportunity-report.
2. Chicano and Latino History Project, "West High School Walkouts," https://latinohistoryproject.org/topic/denver-west-high-school-walkouts/.
3. Colorado Department of Education, "School/District Staff Statistics," accessed April 24, 2024, https://www.cde.state.co.us/cdereval/staffcurrent.
4. Van T. Lac, "The Critical Educators of Color Pipeline: Leveraging Youth Research to Nurture Future Critical Educators of Color," *Urban Review* 51, no. 5 (December 2019): 845–67, https://doi.org/10.1007/s11256-019-00507-4.

Chapter 8

1. Linda Liebenberg, Aliya Jamal, and Janice Ikeda, *Analysing Data with Youth: A Guide to Conducting Thematic Analysis* (Halifax, NS: Spaces and Places, Dalhousie University, 2015), https://youthspacesandplaces.org/wp-content/uploads/2015/09/Spaces-and-Places-Data-Analysis-Manual.pdf; Shepherd Zeldin, Libby Bestul, and Jane Powers, "Practical and Engaging Data Analysis Strategies," in *Youth-Adult Partnerships in Evaluation* (Ithaca, NY: ACT for Youth Center of Excellence, Cornell University, 2012), 30–32, https://fyi.extension.wisc.edu/youthadultpartnership/files/2012/10/Data-Analysis_YAP-Resource-Guide.pdf; Linda Liebenberg, Aliya Jamal, and Janice Ikeda, "Extending Youth Voices in a Participatory Thematic Analysis Approach," *International Journal of Qualitative Methods* 19 (June 2020), https://doi.org/10.1177/1609406920934614.

Chapter 10

1. Dane Stickney and Julissa Ventura, "Possibilities of Student Voice," *Phi Delta Kappan* 105, no. 8 (May 2024): 14–19, https://kappanonline.org/possibilities-of-student-voice.

2. "Visual Analytics: Families, Types, and Importance," Tableau, https://www.tableau.com/data-insights/reference-library/visual-analytics.

Chapter 12

1. Aaron Schutz and Marie G. Sandy, *Collective Action for Social Change: An Introduction to Community Organizing* (New York: Palgrave Macmillan, 2011), 194.

Chapter 14

1. John Bell, *Understanding Adultism: A Major Obstacle to Developing Positive Youth-Adult Relationships* (Somerville, MA: YouthBuild USA, March 1995), https://actioncivics.scoe.net/pdf/Understanding_Adultism.pdf; Melanie Bertrand and Brian D. Lozenski, "YPAR Dreams Deferred? Examining Power Bases for YPAR to Impact Policy and Practice," *Educational Policy* 37, no. 2 (March 2023, published online June 2021): 437–62, https://doi.org/10.1177/08959048211019975; Jerusha O. Conner, C. Nathan Ober, and Amanda S. Brown, "The Politics of Paternalism: Adult and Youth Perspectives on Youth Voice in Public Policy," *Teachers College Record* 118, no. 8 (August 2016): 1–48, https://doi.org/10.1177/016146811611800805; Amy Hillier and Kel Kroehle, "'I'll Save You a Seat': Negotiating Power in a Participatory Action Research Project with Queer and Trans Young Adults," *Urban Education* 58, no. 10 (December 2023, published online June 2021): 2598–627, https://doi.org/10.1177/00420859211023106.
2. Bell, *Understanding Adultism*; Bertrand and Lozenski, "YPAR Dreams"; Conner, Ober, and Brown, "Politics of Paternalism"; Hillier and Kroehle, "'I'll Save You a Seat.'"
3. Bell, *Understanding Adultism*.
4. Bertrand and Lozenski, "YPAR Dreams."
5. Ben Kirshner et al., "Studying Up: How School and District Leaders Interpret Youth Participatory Action Research" (unpublished manuscript, 2024).
6. Kirshner et al., "Studying Up."
7. Angela Booker, "Contingent Authority and Youth Influence: When Youth Councils Can Wield Influence in Public Institutions," *Revista de Investigación Educativa* 35, no. 2 (June 2017): 537–62, https://doi.org/10.6018/rie.35.2.274841.
8. Bertrand and Lozenski, "YPAR Dreams."

Chapter 15

1. Shelley Zion, Ben Kirshner, and Carlos P. Hipolito-Delgado, *Transformative Student Voice: Partnering with Young People for Equitable School Improvement* (Cambridge, MA: Harvard Education Press, forthcoming 2025).

Chapter 16

1. Adapted from Dane Stickney, "My Other Me: Cultivating Student Voice in the Classroom" (PhD diss., University of Colorado Denver, 2022).

2. Carlos P. Hipolito-Delgado et al., "Transformative Student Voice for Sociopolitical Development: Developing Youth of Color as Political Actors," *Journal of Research on Adolescence* 32, no. 3 (September 2022): 1098–1108, https://doi.org/10.1111/jora.12753.

Chapter 17

1. Martin Luther King, Jr., *The Autobiography of Martin Luther King, Jr.*, ed. Clayborne Carson (New York: Warner Books, 1998), 324.
2. Richard Healey and Sandra Hinson, *The Three Faces of Power* (Berkeley, CA: Grassroots Policy Project, 2021), https://grassrootspowerproject.org/analysis/the-three-faces-of-power/.
3. Steven Lukes, *Power: A Radical View,* 2nd ed. (New York: Palgrave Macmillan, 2005).
4. Therese Quinn and Erica R. Meiners, "Queer Kinks and the Arc of Justice: Meditations on Failure, Persistence, and Public Education," *Critical Military Studies* 5, no. 3 (2019, published online May 2018): 238–56, https://doi.org/10.1080/23337486.2018.1464289.
5. Shelley Zion, Ben Kirshner, and Carlos P. Hipolito-Delgado, *Transformative Student Voice: Partnering with Young People for Equitable School Improvement* (Cambridge, MA: Harvard Education Press, forthcoming 2025).

Acknowledgments

We would like to thank the following people who played critical roles as researchers and educators with the TSV research group:

Adam York, Elizabeth Mendoza, Rita Tracy, Carrie Allen, Erin Allaman, Daniela DiGiacomo, Mónica González Ybarra, Erik Dutilly, Kareem Kalil, Melissa Campanella, Laura-Elena Porras Holguin, Montserrat Estrada Martin, Joanna Mendy, Julissa Ventura, Ginnie Logan, Solicia Lopez, Nina Walker, Beatrice Carey Carter, Jessica Neuman, Bill Rozycki, Charles Barnes, Jordana Simmons, Lorena Silva de Andrade Dias, Janelle Alexander, Eshe Price, Dan Tulino, Sharada Krishnamurthy, Scott Oswald, and Jaime Ramge.

A special thank you to Beatriz Salazar, who helped us write two of the chapters in this book. You have been a key part of the TSV team. Your knowledge of ethnic studies, experience with testimonio and other forms of research, and dedication to supporting young people and their educators are invaluable. We wouldn't have such a rich group without you!

While our IRB protocols require that we maintain the anonymity of the teachers and students we support, we wouldn't have a book without their courageous work and willing partnership. It would be easier to just teach the curriculum given. It would be easier to keep researchers outside the classroom. It would be easier as a student to sit, head down, and not engage in schooling. It would be easier to not engage in reflection and just keep doing school the same way. The teachers and students described in this book rejected *easy* at every turn and instead did the difficult but rewarding work of contextualizing a classroom around problems that matter to the students inside of it and then moving forward. And they did it all while being observed, interviewed, and surveyed by the TSV team of researchers. We deeply thank you for being such brave, inviting, and inspiring teachers and students.

Dane, specifically, would like to thank his parents, Gary and Lana Stickney, who were lifelong public educators in Kearney, Nebraska. Dane resisted being a teacher, but the familial pull, thankfully, proved too much. He would also like to thank his wife, Alison, who has taught grades 2–6, served as an assistant principal, and is now in higher ed, for providing the space and support to take on creative ventures like this. He would like to thank his children, Rye, Paige, and Satch, for being daily reminders of the power that young people possess. He would also like to specifically thank Ben Kirshner, Carlos Hipolito-Delgado, and Shelley Zion not only for coauthoring this book but for continually offering career support, mentoring, and opportunities.

Funders

Research reported in this book took place over many years and was supported at different times with grants from the following entities: the Spencer Foundation, the Hewlett Foundation, the William T. Grant Foundation, the American Educational Research Association, and the US Department of Education. The views expressed are those of the authors and do not necessarily reflect the views of the research funders.

We also acknowledge each other. The journey of this book started when Dane, a teacher, took a class from Ben, Carlos, and Shelley, who were then all untenured, early career scholars. We've grown individually and collectively during the past fifteen years, but the journey has taken place in community, which makes it especially powerful.

About the Authors

DANE STICKNEY worked as a newspaper reporter in Colorado, Nebraska, and Iowa for over a decade before becoming a sixth-grade writing teacher at a middle school on Denver's Northside. He and his students tackled social justice topics including undocumented student access to higher education, gentrification, and school-related gun protections while also achieving the district's top scores in writing assessments. After five years in the classroom, Dane moved to the University of Colorado Denver, where he is assistant teaching professor of education supporting teacher development through the ASPIRE to Teach program, the Curriculum and Instruction master's track, and the Student Voice and Leadership initiative through Denver Public Schools. He has been a member of the Transformative Student Voice research collective for a decade and chairs the Action Research Network of the Americas' (ARNA) Youth Participatory Action Research subgroup. His work earned him the 2022 CU Denver campus-wide Service and Leadership award (IRC) and ARNA's Eduardo Flores leadership award in 2024. Dane earned his PhD in 2022; his dissertation focuses on ideas of student voice, teacher agency, and sociopolitical development.

BEN KIRSHNER is a professor of learning sciences and human development at the University of Colorado Boulder. His experiences working with young people at a community center in San Francisco's Mission District motivated his research agenda focused on young people's critical consciousness and their roles leading social justice change. Ben works collaboratively with educators, community organizers, graduate students, and youth to design and study learning environments that support youth development, activism, and civic participation. In his work with the Transformative Student Voice research group (along with Shelley Zion and Carlos Hipolito-Delgado), Ben develops research-practice partnerships that increase public schools' capacity to support student voice and agency through teacher professional learning, policy alignment, and improvement research (www.TransformativeStudentVoice.net). With the Research Hub for Youth Organizing he codesigns educational tools and research studies with youth organizing groups and networks that build capacity for young people to influence policy and public narratives (www.colorado.edu/education-research-hub/). His book, *Youth Activism in an Era of Education Inequality*, received the Social Policy award for best authored book from the Society for Research on Adolescence. Ben has also published in journals that include *Journal of the Learning Sciences, Journal of Research on Adolescence, Applied Developmental Science, Journal of Community Psychology,* and *Cognition and Instruction*.

CARLOS P. HIPOLITO-DELGADO is a professor of counseling at the University of Colorado Denver. His research focuses on the sociopolitical development of students of color, the ethnic identity development of Chicane/x and Latine/x youth, and the cultural competence of counselors. He has been co-principal investigator on grants from the Spencer Foundation, the Hewlett Foundation, KnowledgeWorks, and the American Educational Research Association—all focusing on the sociopolitical development of youth and Transformative Student Voice. Through this grant work he has collaborated on the development of assessments of the quality of youth civic performances and the impact of civics curriculum on academic engagement, civic engagement, and sociopolitical development. He has also published on the use of empowerment and sociopolitical development to foster academic engagement and promote educational reform for marginalized communities. He is past president of the Association for Multicultural Counseling and Development (AMCD) and past chair of the American Counseling Association Foundation. He has been recognized with the Exemplary Diversity Leadership award by AMCD and the University of Colorado Denver Faculty Assembly Excellence in Leadership and Service award.

SHELLEY ZION is a professor of urban education at Rowan University and principal investigator of the PEER (Partnerships for Educational Equity and Research) lab. In this role, she coaches leaders and leads training, research, and community partnerships focused on issues of access, success, and equity. Shelley's team seeks to understand how institutions, social systems, and individual experiences create and sustain systems of power and privilege that ensure access for some while excluding others. Her research is situated within a framework of sociopolitical development, informed by a range of critical theoretical perspectives, and advanced by an understanding of the nature of both individual and systemic change. This framework requires that to impact a transformation of the current public education and other social systems toward goals of equity and social justice, we must work to disrupt dominant ideologies by creating spaces in which people begin to develop a critical understanding of the cultural, political, economic, and other institutional forces that perpetuate systems of privilege and oppression. We must work to develop a critical consciousness, reflective practice, and commitment to action in relation to institutional structures, policies, and practices, and transform those systems toward healing historical wounds, dismantling oppressive systems, and creating equitable access to opportunity. This work requires that education leaders, faculty, staff, community members, and students come together to design new ways of thinking about public school.

Index